What people are say

Trees are our Letters

In *Trees are our Letters*, Carol Day skilfully re-connects us with our sacred relationship with trees. She helps us remember that, as in any relationship, we need to listen. Carol teaches us how to sit with trees to listen again to their language, which is the language of myth. We have become less accustomed to the language of myth. Carol teaches us the letters of this language so that we can decipher it anew for ourselves. Learning this language opens many new doors for us and lets us hear the ancient stories and their wisdom.

Alis Ballance, storyteller and founder of Seanchas, an organisation to keep alive the stories, songs and ancient healing traditions of the Scottish Highlands

Trees are our Letters offers the reader a wonderful exploration of how trees intrinsically weave healing into our lives when we take the time to experience their magic. Weaving tree lore with a step by step guide for self-discovery and exploration Carol offers a gateway into a better understanding of our inner selves. She gently guides the reader through a journey with each tree, offering a template of exploration that connects with the trees through the senses. *Trees are our Letters* is a wonderful journey with trees that provides opportunities for a deeper understanding of connection with nature and the self.

Maureen Phillip, Creativity and Inclusion Director and Multi-Sensory Story Practitioner, PAMIS (promoting a more inclusive society)

On this pilgrimage with the trees, Carol opens up the magic of Inner Landscape supported by the wholeness template of Nature. This carefully crafted journey allows the reader to connect their physical & spiritual senses with the power and presence of trees. This book is a unique and creative way to gain a deeper understanding of oneself and our innate place within Nature's extraordinary landscape.

Rhonda McCrimmon, Founder – The Centre for Shamanism

What a wonderful book about tree appreciation, embracing science and folklore, healing qualities and connection all at once. Carol Day perfectly demonstrates how we are part of nature, and how everything in life is connected. *Trees are our Letters* appreciates the give and take relationship of humans with nature, and that we are not different to nature but an important part of the bigger symbiosis. A very reader friendly language, this book goes deep, yet stays accessible and is perfect for practitioners and for very personal use, growth and learning alike! Thank you, Carol, for such a unique addition for the tree book lover!

Anna Neubert-Wood, Tree lover, Forestbathing facilitator and Founder/Director of Wander Women Scotland Ltd

Our collective disconnection with Nature is seeping into our awareness. It is time to listen with hearts open, to heal and stand in partnership once again with the trees. Rooted and booted, to walk the Earth's robe with humility and respect. Carol Day's beautiful, timely book, is an emissary for the woodlands postal service. Heartsong of the standing ones. Read these letters, then re-read, again and again. Go dreaming with the trees!

Maxine Smillie – Wildwooder, Shamanic Teacher, singer of songs, who can always be found with acorns in her handbag...

Having engaged with small children in the woods for a good many years now, with the support of Carol's Nature as Teacher curriculum, carefully co crafted with our dear departed Cathy

Bache, I found the *Trees are our Letters* book as full of magic as I could have hoped for. Carol writes of a deep connection with trees, of opening our hearts and minds to the richness that flows from root to leaf. The history and lore that travels through time to be with us now as it has always been before us, unfolds in this wonderful opportunity to converse with the trees, to be held and for us to offer our holding. Stepping into true nature connection, one which resounds with the message of truth and creative flow offers positivity and powerful healing to the reader. Carol, thank you for this opportunity, I can't wait to meet more trees!
Kath Webster, Nature Connection facilitator for small people

Carol Day's book inspires us to take a journey with our Tree relations and deepen our relationship with them and their stories. As the tree beings have generously offered their teachings and insights to Carol, so with reciprocity at the heart of her book, she inspires us to re connect to our mythical as well as physical world through them, planting seeds for the future wellbeing of all.
Claire Hewitt, Storyteller, and author of *Tree Stories*, a Scottish Forestry Commission Outdoor Learning publication

In *Trees are our Letters*, Carol takes us by the hand and leads us through the world of ten trees encouraging us to build a relationship with each tree and ourselves. Opening our hearts to our creativity, opening ourselves to nature by listening to and learning from the trees. Connecting with each aspect of the tree from root through to seeds and each aspect of ourselves; learning from the trees will in turn teach us so much about ourselves.

Carol sets out the formular of working with the trees so clearly and beautifully. The secret of each tree that she shares with the reader is simply a starting point to set us off on our own journey of discovery.

The timing of this book is perfect, arriving at a time when stopping to listen and learn from the lands around us is

imperative, to find our way forward into a "new normal".
Lyn Hill, Founder of Sacred Awakenings

Trees are our Letters is a beautifully written and illustrated book reflecting on ten trees and the ways we can meet them to help us in our Visionary journeys, whether we are new to the practice, or wish to refresh our existing work. Carol Day writes about the uses, history and mythology of each tree and gives the reader clear and helpful exercises to awaken and enhance their inner sight, their spirituality and healing. And each reader can decide for themselves how they wish to use the book, from being drawn to work with a particular tree for its special qualities, to working through the book as a journey of spiritual development. In an era when so many have forgotten the power of nature and its many lessons for our wellbeing, this is indeed a healing and inspiring book, to be read by the novice and practised Visionary alike. It deserves a wide readership.
Jane Hill, modern mystic, author of *Six Enchantments*

There is a feeling I get when I sit with a wise, majestic tree. It is one of steady grounding, rootedness and being held in a blanket of wisdom and love. It is that same feeling as I am working through *Trees are our Letters*. Somehow Carol has managed to transfer the magic of the trees into something I can use to expand and deepen my connection with them. The book is a wonderful companion both for those new to the mysteries the trees hold for us as well as offering new possibilities and doorways to further adventures for those of us who might already hold the trees as dear friends. It is a book that could be read again and again and each time discover something new and astonishing. A true joy for us and a real gift and honouring of the trees.
Ashleigh Ranft, Founder of Soul Nourishment

Trees are our Letters

A creative appointment with
nature's communicators

Trees are our Letters

A creative appointment with
nature's communicators

Carol Day

MOON
BOOKS

Winchester, UK
Washington, USA

JOHN HUNT PUBLISHING

First published by Moon Books, 2023
Moon Books is an imprint of John Hunt Publishing Ltd., No. 3 East Street, Alresford
Hampshire SO24 9EE, UK
office@jhpbooks.net
www.johnhuntpublishing.com
www.moon-books.net

For distributor details and how to order please visit the 'Ordering' section on our website.

Text copyright: Carol Day 2022

ISBN: 978 1 78099 386 7
978 1 78099 387 4 (ebook)
Library of Congress Control Number: 2021951679

A CIP catalogue record for this book is available from the British Library.

Design: Matthew Greenfield

UK: Printed and bound by CPI Group (UK) Ltd, Croydon, CR0 4YY
Printed in North America by CPI GPS partners

We operate a distinctive and ethical publishing philosophy in
all areas of our business, from our global network of authors to
production and worldwide distribution.

Contents

For Cathy and the Trees

Be taught now, among the trees and rocks,
how the discarded is woven into shelter,
learn the way things hidden and unspoken
slowly proclaim their voice in the world.
Find that far inward symmetry
to all outward appearances, apprentice
yourself to yourself, begin to welcome back
all you sent away, be a new annunciation,
find the words you always wanted to say
and stand at the door of the day
and be hospitable, even to the stranger in you.

David Whyte

Previous Books

Wheel (2017)
978-1-78808-432-1 (Paperback)
978-1-78808-250-1 (e-book)

Drum (2018)
978-1-78808-323-2 (Paperback)
978-1-78808-324-9 (e-book)

Story Compass (2022)
978-1-78904-850-6 (Paperback)
978-1-78904-851-3 (e-book)

Acknowledgements

I would like to acknowledge two counties in the British Isles, with their trees and their people.

Firstly, Yorkshire! The childhood I had with the trees there has made me who I am. It has kept me always knowing how deep my roots are and taught me how deep and wondrous the worlds these trees open doors to are. I also want to acknowledge my mum, Ann, who one day nonchalantly just let it slip that she hears trees singing all the time! I am not that cool! But I salute you and all our ancestors who have this gift to speak with nature and passed it down the line.

Secondly, I acknowledge Fife: the land where I became a mother, firstly to a son and then a daughter. I acknowledge you, Arin and your first word 'duir' which you would say emphatically whenever you wanted me to open something for you. In time, I realised it was the sound of oak that means to open. And so, the ancestors speak on! And to Tsen, for your living between worlds with me and for your fearless climbing of trees to the very tops. You know trees in the highest places!

Fife, thank you for showing me your vision in a mystical experience so I had no choice but to come back and work with the nature spirits there. Thank you, Cathy, my soul friend, now in spirit, for your courageous soul and for the magic that worked between us when we brought through the Nature as Teacher model with the trees for your vision: the Secret Garden Outdoor nursery. To all the friends, inspiring people, students and communities in Fife that have been built in nature over these years through the families around the nursery; the Theatre of Dragon Hill in Wormit; the little red drum and then the Creative Vision project in Falkland, with my second family, the Mckeens; the Centre for Stewardship and the clear and tree loving ancestors of the land, who taught me slowly how to remember ways to include everyone and everything again.

They say if you want to master, teach. I taught this work to save my life because when I nearly got thrown out of my body, what I could mainly hear from then on were the sounds of nature and the spirits. I couldn't send them away for they had been waiting so patiently for someone to see and weave with them. Besides, the world of humans was so dull now I saw what was missed out. So, I had to find a way to find the others who saw them too. In time we gathered ourselves to listen to the vision of the land and the trees and to uncover a way. I see you all. We are a part of something wondrous and true and the trees lead the way.

Lastly, thank you Fay, for the incredible soul that you are and for writing such a perfect Foreword for this book.

Preface

I am crouching beneath the pendulous branches of the birch tree at the bottom of my garden. I am crouching because I want my body to be in the sun and my laptop in the shade as I type! In my line of vision, I see the rope ladder attached to our tree for us to climb into the natural seat it provides. I think about the ladders these trees and the stories of trees open worlds to. Pondering the subject of how to write a preface for a book and the question 'What kind of folk am I hoping this book will reach?' I decide to post my enquiry to the tree. Intuitively I receive the answer 'All the ordinary people'.

Trees are our Letters is a book that will take any ordinary person on a writing retreat with the trees. The trees and your availability to be present for and with them are the teachers! I have written a book and a programme that can be accessed by children, teenagers and adults of all ages, and especially for people who are interested in opening up to their writing skills and creativity alongside nature. I am hoping that the end product of your working with this book will be the living of a deeper connection between you and nature and an entry into new creative ways of writing and living. Beyond that you and the trees are in charge!

Ordinary people and ordinary trees want to be linked together again. *Trees are our Letters* is a truth that comes from one of the ancient systems of writing in which each tree sound has formed the vowel or consonant sounds of most of the English language. It seemed perfectly ordinary for me to write a book that would give space for this original language to connect us back with the trees and all the other things the trees are so good at connecting with.

Your author is an artist and an educator. I went to art college to study art and then I got so into trying to understand how art and its communication systems worked that I went on to learn primary school education and find out from the masters of creativity themselves: young children. Most of what I have learnt about connection has been through my own disconnect and through observing and working with children. My mantra is that play is the best way to learn and playing in nature is the best way to reconnect and open. I really want this book to help all the ordinary people like me and you and everyone to play again!

Trees are our Letters is an informative, creative, soulful and meditative journey with ten of our planet's species of trees. It can be picked up and opened at any page and you can take your time. Or, it can be worked through as a pilgrimage treat for yourself in your everyday life as one hundred days with ten trees. You will find yourself writing prose, poetry, the beginnings to a novel, short stories, songs, recipes and all manner of things on the journey! You will emerge with ten new loyal tree friends, sturdy in character and unique in the gifts and counselling they bring, who I am sure will open the doors to make you want to befriend many more!

This book is a book written by a community.

In friendship,

Carol and the ten trees

Foreword

Trees. Not referred to as large plants, but rooted in our language with their very own noun, trees. That tells you something doesn't it? It hints to me that there is something more than meets the eye with trees. The source of our oxygen, shelter and habitats for our wildlife, trees are a vital component of our delicate ecosystem. Yet what alchemists the largest plants on our planet are. Trees ingeniously transform sunlight, water and micronutrients into solid matter. Creative beings that continuously create our landscape whether or not we are present to this magic.

In my childhood I looked upon these green giants with wonder. My first tree friends were the apple trees at the bottom of the garden. There was a wobbly old rope ladder attached to one of the branches. I felt so daring when I climbed up. I also remember a hammock of sorts strung up between the two trees and swinging with a girlfriend in our early teens sharing our growing pains and giggling endlessly. These trees witnessed me, they held the space while I grew, while our family grew together and found its way. They saw the fun we had and they heard the battles. They held space, not just for us, but for the owners before us and the family that came thirty years after. In my stillness I can still feel them and conjure a sense of their presence. In my body I can feel the gentle bob of the tree as it sinks down to hold my weight on the ladder and hear the rustle of the leaves and branches that move in response. The tartness of a cooking apple or the smoothness of its bright green skin brings them all back through the doorways of my heart. The apple brings me a sense of homely comfort, innocence and exploration, adventure and magic. In fact, this feeling is always there for me whenever I am with an apple tree.

Trees are the longest living species on our planet, linking us to the past, present and future. They are as much a part of our inner landscape as they are our external environment. Don't think that living in a city makes you immune. Lone trees linger on street corners even in the most urban environments with their canopies reaching up high through the stratosphere and their roots travelling far and wide through the earth. The forests communicate with each other, science shows us that now, and I know they have quite a story to tell.

When did you last play and lose yourself in nature? When did you last pause, reach out and touch a tree to experience it for yourself and meet it as an intelligent being? Many of us have lost or forgotten the habit of immersing ourselves in nature and marvelling at its beauty. This is why with Carol showing us the way in this book, we can rekindle this innate ability and remember how to reconnect.

With this book Carol expertly guides us and playfully encourages us to reach out and connect to ten different trees. She lays out a unique structure which is easy to follow and invites you to meet the tree with an eager and childlike playful attitude. It's in this way that you can step through the invisible portal and meet the tree not just with your physical senses but with the creative, intuitive all-knowing parts of you that are your truth.

While the book does share facts about a tree's history and identification, the focus is your interaction and experience with the tree. These exercises encourage you to create your own impression of each tree and form a unique relationship with the green being to discover the specific quality it awakens within you. Along the way there is healing, meditation and opportunity to journey into the tree and emerge transformed in some way after your encounter.

In my experience with plants, they always choose us. The trees haven't been chosen from a list, they've been selected as Carol was guided to them as part of her endless work to restore wholeness as Visionary, artist and educator.

Reading this book, I think fondly of all the times I have sat in circle with Carol Day as my way shower, knowing I am held safely in a compassionate space. I remember venturing into nature guided by Carol to meet the magic that lay waiting. In my experience there is always an opening to a deeper understanding, a release like a long-needed exhalation and a settling into a new way of being, seeing and feeling.

I have no doubt that if you meet even just one of the trees in this book by following the map carefully laid out by Carol, that your life will be transformed. A shift will occur, perhaps a new tree friend will be made, perhaps the cloak you have been wearing that blocks your light will be lifted, perhaps you will simply feel seen as if the subtle veil that envelops your world has rippled outwards and you can take a deep breath of fresh air. Words and images may flow, a new rhythm will begin to unfold and it's definitely worth the adventure. Your tree teachers are waiting with their letters to create your new story.

Fay Johnstone, author of *Plants that Speak, Souls that Sing* and *Plant Spirit Reiki*

May 2021

Introduction

How many times have you felt out of kilter and then gone out to the woods or walked by a river lined with trees, only to find that how you have been feeling can vanish or be met and held by these gracious earthly companions? How many times have you felt cooped up and bored only to brace the storms outside your window and encounter a steady tree trunk that you are drawn to crouch beside then seamlessly find your way back to aliveness again? Have you ever driven down a carriageway in late May or early June and had your heart burst open by the hawthorn blossom waving their stems in the hazy dusk of spring? Have you watched with anticipation the Cherry blossom as they come through each day in your garden and wondered why you feel so darned happy? Or maybe you have had *that* event, the one that has felt too much to bear, that you don't want to bring others down by mentioning and also even though everyone knows about it, still no one mentions it? Later, you will find yourself carrying all of this unbearable weight out to climb a hill and making a stop in time to lean your entire weight against a solid tree, crying or screaming with your whole might at the wind. After a while, pausing, you look around and find yourself going 'Wait, what? This actually doesn't dent the tree? Hey, really? The tree is actually listening to me here? It is able to hold me? Are you honestly really there tree?' A profound silence ensues. A deep meeting of souls begins, never to be forgotten and from now on, here for eternity. The trees are there for us.

Myself, I am quite a drama being. I feel moods intensely. I am potato-like. Get ready for my interpretation of potato! For me the potato is earthy and quite plain in just wanting to belong as part of a natural world, yet it is wide open to osmosis. (Do you remember those osmosis experiments with potatoes in the labs at school? Do they still do them?) Like the process of osmosis, I can assimilate anything it would seem, unconsciously. All kinds of traumas and feelings can soak in and be felt deeply. This means I have had to work hard over the years to find ways to avoid this absorption unnecessarily and to deal with it when it happens. My favourite tactic is to get outdoors to be with the trees and the wind and with them find my station again. What an ingenious game my body, mind and feelings play to get me out where I truly belong! Does this ring bells for you? Have you been finding that trees reach the parts that humans just can't seem to reach?

I have this theory about humans I use a lot when teaching Visionary work. Humans are shape shifters and mergers. Humans pick up on feelings. We take on impressions; copy others; can absorb programmes, soak up atmospheres; ride out the emotions of theatre, films and books; get driven by media stories and live our lives as if in the place of other folk sometimes. My grandmother used to talk with me about the characters on *Neighbours* or *Home and Away* as if they were our friends. I find myself years later watching a screen and waking up referencing myself against life in the Eighteenth Century of *Outlander*. You would never find a dog, tulip, clay soil or magpie acting like this. It seems that our community in nature get on with the job of being just what they are. I suspect in doing this they are also getting on with the amazing experience of intercommunicating with everything else on this planet and beyond as well. Perhaps we are missing out a lot of what it is to be here because of our unconscious merging and shape shifting ways?

But what would it be like then to all be conscious about this way of being together? I mean, did you know – this is the realm of the magician and the seer, our human gift to naturally pick up on something and then to enact or act upon it! We have the ability to pick up on and feel for the whole of nature and partake in the intercommunication at play. We also have the added human advantage of being able to socially meet and discuss what we are feeling or perceiving and create something wondrous as a way of life. We could get soul to soul with the trees and then put something into action that was for the trees and for us.

Well, this is kind of where this book is going. It is a book that will help you to open up the abilities you have and then go off with the trees to help you to learn about yourself and the trees at the same time. Then it is getting you to work creatively with the trees as a joint writing or words project.

Trees are our Letters is a journey of one hundred days with the trees as our teachers! Its pages bring a potential of reconnection, surprise, creative flow and a deepening of your understanding of your role on earth. This book is a tried and tested journey into the Visionary realms of trees and humans!

You can work with this book in a number of ways. You could choose to work with each tree in turn and set aside a period of your life to go through this bardic journey. You might instead feel to work with a chapter when you find one of the trees drawing your attention. Or, you could just dip in and out of the material exactly as you wish. Opening this book initiates a path of listening to yourself and listening to nature even more truly. So, feel the permission to choose to go with your flow from the onset. It will see you well. The path will take you into the worlds of ten major trees and set up healing pathways with each tree and their medicine. As Visionary workers (a bit more about that in a moment), we have deep connections with the nature realms. This book will bring this connection even more to the fore.

Trees hold clear stations for us in the natural world. They can be felt as guardians for us and the planet. What you will find reading through this material is that the more each of us can allow ourselves to come into synch with our true nature, then the more we will find the trees standing there resolutely to guide us. *Trees are out Letters* is designed to create opportunities for you to step into your place in nature and to access major gateways through getting closer to some of the members of our planet's amazing tree dynasties.

So, let's begin by speaking a bit about the ethos of this book and laying some foundations for the rich exploration to follow.

Hopes

My hope is that you will be able to make your own unique connection with trees and that this will open up great qualities within you. The vision held is that the trees will also feel the web being opened as more and more people actively plug into this connection and so an alliance can happen. It is that the web of life can benefit from this connection being opened and that the story fields of life can stretch back to fully accommodate the language and important alliance of trees with humans again.

Structuring

Here is how the book is structured:

There are ten chapters: one for each tree as well as this introduction and an epilogue. The material in each tree chapter is organised as follows.

Roots: This is the lore and it gives you information on the qualities that the tree you are working with you is renowned for holding.

Trunk: Here is a practice for you to set up working with your everyday senses with the tree.

Branches: Here are pathways you can take with the tree opening up whilst spending time with it or whilst accessing the realms behind this one in a journey.

Leaves: This is a healing exercise you can access with the tree that works with the intention you bring to the book.

Seeds: Here you take the seeds from the tree to seed your own creativity through story.

This structure is repeated throughout and this brings simplicity to the following of the journey with each tree. I recommend approximately three hours per chapter of dedicated time to follow the material and be with the tree (in body or spirit!) and to write.

Ten trees
These are the ten trees to be your teachers for the book!

Sycamore
Beech
Cedar
Poplar
Magnolia
Cherry
Elm
Horse Chestnut
Hornbeam
Sequoia

Information

Read through the following passages before we begin. The information is designed to support you to understand the nature of the Visionary and the philosophy of creativity the book works with. Reading this will prepare you for the material working with the trees and will acquaint you with some of the terms and practices that come up. At the end of this section there is a checklist of things to do before you embark on your meetings with the trees!

Why *Trees are our Letters*? What a great question! The answer lies in the Ogham!

Ogham

The Ogham is the rudiments of an ancient alphabet whose letters come from the sounds for different trees. These letters became integrated in the later developing Latin speech sounds and symbols we use in the English/American and many other European languages today. We speak and write with the letters of the trees. How cool is that?

The Ogham is a druidic alphabet. It consists of twenty characters that are the trees and their sounds. The characters are simple and easily drawn using downward and upward strokes and probably would have been conveyed as hand signals too.

Most of the trees in *Trees are our Letters* are different to these trees, but the Ogham serves to show how fundamental the trees are to our innate communication systems.

Visionary (think Listener!)

I wonder if you can imagine a world where everything listens and everything is listened to. Could you imagine a world in which the natural balance of everything is cared for first and foremost? This would be a world of inclusion: A world where anything that aches or anything that tries to remove itself is allowed the space that it needs.

Can you visualise a world where it is understood that

everything has a spirit, a place and a way of communicating? What do you think it would be like if we could find ways to communicate with absolutely everything? Can you imagine a life open to allowing and understanding different frequencies and expressions? Think how you could sit with a tree, understand its nature and feel its support.

Imagine what it would be like if we could begin to see the different communication paths as we each opened up to be able to communicate with more and more. Can you picture how by opening up to more we were each able to feel our load lifted? This could mean that we could each see our own guiding systems and ourselves so much more easily.

Imagine if we could know exactly where to go for support at the moment we sensed we needed it. How would it be to wake up every morning and focus on what could be created and enjoyed? Imagine that ease and brilliance!

The Listener holds this vision. The listener today is no different to the first people. We have always known this way of considering the wholeness. It is what is true. Everything we do in this listening way, we do to restore this template and click it back into place. The Listener is the intelligent compass and is the part of each of us who remembers the connected, balanced way of being and carries the pulse of inter-connectedness everywhere we go. I call this the Visionary nature. The Visionary nature can bring the outer world back into balance again!

Nature

The secret of holding the Visionary nature is to allow our true innate nature to shine. By transferring the usage of the word nature to that within, it can show how the world of nature around us is key to guiding us back to this. Here is a piece about how nature works:

The natural world has a rhythm and an order that is in tune with the cyclical nature of life and the seasons. As the earth and the other planets of our solar system circle our sun and our moon circles the earth to create seasonal changes and moon cycles, nature grows and moves along in accordance with this. To allow ourselves to be first and foremost a part of nature, all we need to do as humans is to readjust our focus and let ourselves respond in the connective way that nature responds and behaves.

This grid of interconnectivity is the field of nature that is the natural order of everything. I sometimes refer to this as the wholeness template.

By responding to the natural order and cyclical nature, we can discover what is known as optimum flow. Our life becomes easier as we click into a supportive cycle where all our projects and experiences are those of opening and closing, birthing, growing and dying. Learning to listen to nature and the resonant life on our planet through the constant arcs of the seasonal cycles means that we can connect deeply with the life force and the intelligence in all of life. The trees are major guides and guardians for us in this restorative project, loyally leading us in!

Forces and Play

Coming to a place where we can fully own our elemental nature as a fact and a reality brings us to the place of being able to accept and engage with the power of our Visionary nature.

Journeying back through time to the beginnings of the universe and the creation of life, it is the dark, the light and the elements that we discover. The force of the elements is the primal force of nature and of our selves. The elements move through us and the powerful fact is that, essentially, we are they.

The word archetype is taken from the Greek words *arkhe* and *tupos* that mean original and model. The archetypes are the original models of elemental patterns set in nature and also of course in human motivation and behaviour. We can see ourselves as being orchestrated by the power of these archetypal forces. We can see our work as humans as being about harnessing and directing these forces with intention and care.

Each tree has a special relationship with these archetypal forces and carries a story that supports healing along the lines of this archetype. We will meet each these forces and stories working with each tree as we go along.

The Power of Presence and the
Effect of the Observer

Presence is key to listening's effectiveness! When we are present with what is, we engage with wholeness and step out of our separated notion of self. We can then move into a place where we can see clearly our Visionary within.

Nature helps us to restore this power of presence. Nature doesn't think and analyse. So, when we are in nature, we can attune to the frequency of being again.

Animals and the electromagnetic waves of the earth operate in the alpha range. Yogis see the alpha state as the rhythm of nature. Our brains generally vibrate at between fourteen and twenty-one cycles per second. These brain waves are known as beta waves. In this state we are attentive and focused on everyday external activities.

Alpha waves vibrate at seven to fourteen waves per second. With our brains in alpha state, we enter a relaxed state of well being.

In the trance state of drumming, the brain waves of humans move into the alpha and then into the slower theta and maybe delta ranges in deep trance. Theta waves vibrate at four to seven cycles per second and are threshold of sleep dreamy state. Delta waves are one to four cycles per second. They are deep sleep and the brains of foetuses emit delta waves. You can see from this how the shaman nature is more in the other worlds – like in sleep and pre-birth – when the frequency of the brain waves go so slow. You can see how revelatory information can come through and the potential for healing change is reached.

This is why when we go for a walk in nature inspirations can come. We move into a state of being where we are open to the bigger picture coming through to guide us.

How we view something affects everything. There are variables in what reality is according to the conditions that are present. The Observer effect considered through early quantum experiments by Heisenberg in the 1920s has influenced lots of speculation on this matter. Paradoxes like Wigner's Friend come in with experiments looking at whether the observer being watched affects the experiment too. The same set of experiments spurred tests for ascertaining whether reality actually exists until it is viewed: A particle is only a wave without form until it is observed.

When we come to the place of presence and look at life through the eyes of our Visionary nature, so many affecters on the nature of reality can become apparent.

We exist inside a huge field of effective agents. These effecting agents are connected to the different organisations of life to which we have a belonging. Let's name just a few of them: The body parts and organs, our relationships, the family, our workplaces, politics, the community, our country, our geography, continent, planet, our culture, religion, all of the ancestors, the mythological constructs, archetypal energy, the solar system, the stars. Some of these are natural and stand with of our true nature. Some hold our true nature hostage or limit us.

There are many fields and stories running! You just have to read the media with a detachment and see the scripts at work. All of these fields are having an effect on us at any time. We can feel loyalties and pulls to the forces and expectations within these fields. We can come to recognise that we are actually being affected by a number of belief systems at the same time and that some of these are compromising our ability to feel permission to be in harmony with our own preferences and ways of being.

An exploration of these fields at work can bring much information to the surface, giving potential to free a lot. What we want to end up at is a situation where everyone claims their natural ability to be an authority on themselves and is fully aware and responsible for their own choices and actions.

In this journey of *Trees are our Letters* we are invited by the trees to step into their field and to read the story through their senses.

Story

You will find that this book supports you to weave with story throughout. Story is a connected account or a narration of some happening. A story has a beginning, middle and ending and is what we tell and is what we communicate to ourselves or to another.

Everything carries a story. We put others into our stories. Other people put us into their stories. We have stories that we retell and recount as families, communities and nations. There are certain stories that become very important to certain people.

You can see that stories can be very powerful in the way

that they focus people's attention and how they can bring out upset or inspiration. When we recount a story there can be a strong therapeutic element that is integral with the telling of it. We can feel the act of telling a story sometimes creating a deep bond with another person or a group of people. On entering the reading or hearing of a story, we can find a resonance with our own life experiences. So, stories can help us to process things and set ourselves free.

Without story we wouldn't be here. There would be no relationship between anything. Everything would be wave with no particles. As soon as something comes into relationship with something else, communication happens. The eternal waves become two particles and then more. Consciousness in relationship brings a story into being. You can perhaps see how powerful every particle is in affecting another. Consciously working with this awareness of the power of affect and working with story within life is sacred and healing engineering.

Story is important because it mirrors the way that everything is brought into relationship. When this mirror is placed strategically, creation can be influenced and affected. In *Trees are our Letters* we allow the stories of the trees to come through us. We bring trees into our story and this changes our world.

Visionary Exploration

Visionary exploration is one of the listening practices that can support us to open up to the spirits of the different trees and to intuit and receive information and healing. When we open up to a Visionary exploration, we step out of our beta led self and go deeper into the alpha and slower brain wave state. We drop into the heartbeat of nature and the trees. We access our Visionary nature and the worlds that exist beyond our everyday self. The trees act as guides for this.

Traditionally, trees are renowned for their accessing through portals for journeys into the other worlds. The tree, like the axis mundi of the chakra system in the human body, is known as a bearer of the different frequencies that open up gateways to different states of being. These states are often mapped as the underworld accessed through the roots of the tree, the upper world accessed through the branches and the spiritual aspects of the everyday middle world as the trunk.

You will be recommended to go into a Visionary exploration by sitting with a tree or by holding a part of a tree (e.g. its seeds or branch) in your hand as part of this book. You may also use a drum or rattle to help you to connect as the continuous sound helps you to move into alpha or slower brain waves that will open your mind up to the dreaming space.

The secret is to hold presence. The task below will be something you will repeat every time you go to sit or stand with a tree.

Alignment task with a tree, nature and presence
Find yourself by a tree and sit or stand beside it. Depending on your unique sensory way of being, access each of the following planes of your senses. Listen to all the sounds there are all around you right now. With the tree at your back, allow yourself to ground with the world of sound making.

With your eyes, search out all the visual information around you at this moment in time. Be aware of textures and tones. With the tree at your back, allow yourself to settle for a minute or two with the world of visual form making.

With your sense of smell, search out all the scents in the air around you this time. Be aware of sweet and sour. With the tree at your back, allow yourself to ground for a minute or two with the world of aroma making.

With your sense of touch, feel the form of the tree, its branches and bark and the earth you are both on. Be aware of roughness, smoothness and pattern. With the tree at your back, allow yourself to settle for a minute or two with the world of touchable form making.

With your sense of taste, savour with your tongue anything you feel drawn to (that you know is not poisonous of course). Be aware of the flavours. With the tree at your back, allow yourself to ground for a moment or two with the world of flavour giving.

Now bring attention to yourself as a sensory being in this world. Feel your connection with the world through your senses. Feeling the tree at your back, allow yourself now to connect to the tree as a being. Access a deeper sense to do this. Now feel yourself as a being. Begin to open up to the earth, the sky, the creatures, the grass, all as beings. Stay like this for about ten minutes. Feel your everyday self move into a different space from this cool calm clear earth sense of self.

Let the tree and the earth know you love them as you connect with them and let yourself know you love you and know you are also a part of the earth too.

Instruments for connection and their relationship with trees

The frame drum used by many Visionary traditions is made from a ring of wood from a sacred tree. Sometimes this is a tree that has been struck by lightning. An animal skin or synthetic material is stretched across this. The wood from the tree acts as a hoop through which we can communicate with the other realms. I call this a tree hoop. The skin is a membrane we can tap with a beater to create a vibration that then sounds with the vibration of the world around us. It does this simultaneously with the vibration of the issue we open up to connect with. The drum bearer climbs onto the back of the spirit of the animal the skin is from, or the spirit that is assigned to the drum. The animal carries them to journey into these worlds.

The tree hoop acts as the portal as does the tree we are journeying into at each stage of this book. I recommend you have a frame drum to work with on this training as well as listening to a drumming or steady chanting track.

Lore

Lore is the ancient knowledge that we have had handed down about the trees and it is also the knowledge we can access from the trees today by opening up to working with the trees. You will receive information from lore for each of the trees you will be working with.

Creativity and the Muse

The Visionary nature works with the creative process both to bring healing and to vision the continuing world into being. *Trees are our Letters* opens up pathways to deepen your relationship with creativity.

Here is some information about creativity and the muse:

Integral to the creative process is the power of the muse. The muse is the power that sparks the creative process. The muse is like a power that sparks through the realms and weaves with creation.

The word museum is Latin and is taken from the Greek *mouseion* 'seat of the Muses,' based on *mousa* 'muse.'

The nine muses as a phenomenon in Ancient Greece were the Protectors of the arts. They protected by defining and holding a space and reverence for each of the nine scopes of speciality in Greek civilisation. Each muse helped to bring through the creative spirit of an area of creative development. Many of the early peoples had nine maidens at the core of their mystery schools who looked after different aspects of life too. These nine maidens are a pattern that continues through many traditions.

The nine muses are the daughters of Zeus and Mnemosyne. They are known for the music of their song, which brings joy to any who hear it. Here are their names with an interpretation of their departments: Clio (History), Urania (Astronomy), Melpomene (Tragedy), Thalia (Comedy), Terpsichore (Dance), Calliope (Epic Poetry), Erato (Love Poetry), Polyhymnia (Songs to the Gods), Euterpe (Lyric Poetry).

So, the seat of the muses was the place where one would go to be inspired – much like the function of museums, as we know them today. The spark of divine inspiration we are talking about which was called the muse is inherent in everything.

We can move further back in time to a nature inclusive culture and refer to the early museums as temples in the woods where humans and all other earth-based spirits alike would communicate with the other realms and keep creation flowing in beautiful ways. The trees would have been these early nodes. They continue to be this today! These temples through all times were powerhouses and safe places for the Visionary nature. The Visionary nature was revered and looked after so that the whole of life could remain connected.

I like to think of the nodes and passageways in the communication networks we have in the 21st century. The word node comes from the Latin 'nodus' and means knot. It is a connection point, a redistribution point, or a communication end point in data terminal equipment.

The definition of a node depends on the network and its protocol layer. A physical network node is an active electronic device that is attached to a network. It is capable of creating, receiving, or transmitting information over a communications channel. A passive distribution point such as distribution frame is not a node. A distribution point has to be active to be a node.

The tree groves and these later more decorative centres of creation would hold very special roles for assisting healing energy flow.

One of the things we can do to look after our Visionary nature and revive our connectivity with the power to create and feel our wider nature is to reacquaint ourselves with the trees and the muse.

Setting yourself up to begin

1. Take some time to be with the trees for the days approaching when you will begin the material. You can drum to the trees or you can simply sit or stand in silence with them. Practice the attunement exercise above regularly.

2. Think about your intention for working with *Trees are our Letters*. What are you looking to gain from these one hundred days or more? What are you looking to heal? What would you like to learn? What will be different for you when you complete? Write down your intention. It will lead the way. Put it in a place where you can refer regularly to it.

3. Get yourself a notebook to write words that come from being with the trees and also to make drawings or rubbings. You can simply begin by writing how you are

feeling when you are with the tree. You can move on to write questions for the tree and then intuit answers. You can open up to see if you can bring small poems together.

4. Have a look at the structure you will be working with to acquaint yourself with the process. Free two or more hours in your schedule for each of the days with a new tree.

5. Drum a blessing to the trees and to your intention.

Lots of blessings to you on this journey with the trees!

Chapter 1

Sycamore

Sycamore is one of the sacred trees of Ancient Egypt, its two winged plane seeds representing the Upper and Lower Kingdoms on the Nile and it has origins in the Middle Eastern lands. It grows tall and strong and creates a wide canopy. It was introduced to the UK about six hundred years ago. There are other theories too that it was the Romans who brought the seeds over. The idea of it being brought across by the Crusaders in the Middle Ages as part of a pilgrimage of seeding the sacred tree from Palestine through Europe, England Wales and Scotland speaks of the tree's power.

The Sycamore is a hardy tree. It can also thrive in all kinds of climates, loving acidic soils too. We have an abundance in Scotland. Sycamore is a perfect tree to start us off opening doors from the everyday to the mystical as it holds strong the themes of duality and oneness.

So, remember this structure below is the one you will work with for each tree. Right now, give yourself ten minutes to read through this chapter. I then ask you to spend five minutes quietly attuning or drumming or rattling to ask to connect with the tree in spirit. Feel out into the earth around you for any trees of this species on the land.

Working with Sycamore

First you need to find a Sycamore tree! If you can't reach one easily see if you can take a bit of a branch from a Sycamore you find. You can ask the tree if it is willing to give you a small twig or see if there is one fallen to the ground. You can also work with seeds or leaves or a bit of its bark. Any part of the tree is good. You will now be working through this material with the tree parts to really get to know this tree:

Roots: This is the lore and it gives you information on the qualities that the tree you are working with you is renowned for holding.

Trunk: Here is a practice for you to set up working with your everyday senses with the tree.

Branches: Here are pathways you can take with the tree opening up whilst spending time with it or whilst accessing the realms behind this one in a journey.

Leaves: This is a healing exercise you can access with the tree that works with the intention you bring to the book.

Seeds: Here you take the seeds from the tree to seed your own creativity through story.

Roots
Sycamore's Lore

The botanical name of Sycamore, Acer pseudoplatanus, means

'like a plane tree'. The Sycamore can grow to thirty-five metres high and can live for four hundred years. The bark is dark pink-grey and smooth when young, but becomes cracked and develops small plates with age. Twigs are pink-brown and hairless. Its palmate leaves measure seven to sixteen centimetres and have five lobes. The leaf stalks of younger trees are characteristically red. Its flowers are small, green-yellow and hang in spikes, or 'racemes'. After pollination by wind and insects, female flowers develop into distinctive winged fruits known as samaras. You can notice that leaf veins are hairy on the underside.

Sycamore is attractive to aphids and a variety of their predators like ladybirds, hoverflies and birds. The leaves are eaten by caterpillars of moths, including the Sycamore moth, plumed prominent and maple prominent. The flowers provide a good source of pollen and nectar to bees and other insects. Birds and small mammals consume the seeds.

The Sycamore grows slowly and is slow to mature but with its well-designed helicopter seeds reproduces fruitfully. It is particularly popular for making musical instruments and butcher's blocks. It is a good wood for coppicing and it is reckoned that an average seven acre croft planted with mixed broadleaf high in Sycamore will be self-replenishing and will offer stock shelter and enough fuel for one family for ever.

In Wales, Sycamore trees were used in the traditional craft of making 'love spoons'. The winged seeds are known as 'helicopters', and used in flying competitions and model-making by children.

Sycamore trees have a long history in folklore dating back to Egyptian times where the Holy Sycamore is said to connect the worlds between the dead and the living. This great tree is said to stand at the Eastern gate of heaven, which releases the sun to rise each morning.

Sycamores are renowned for their longevity. The North

American Sycamore can grow to mammoth proportions. Their strangely coloured trunks become mottled with white, grey and greenish brown when the bark flakes off. This can make them seem mysterious. Some of the indigenous people of North America call them 'Ghosts of the Forest'. There are many tales spun around their magical nature. You can see how they can move between the worlds!

Apparently, it was beneath the broad spreading branches of this tree that Mary and Jesus stopped for a breather on the flight into Egypt.

The medicine of Sycamore is to bring patience and curb restlessness. It can increase self-worth and a feeling of being valued to spend time with Sycamore. It can support relationships where one partner grows away from the other and couples who are growing apart can find healing in a Sycamore wood. Sycamore restores the balance within a relationship, between male and female. It can also bring healing of a necessary separation, where the separation is healthy and necessary for the soul's progression. It can help to bring understanding and independence and stop blame. It is said to be good for people whose roots are in a different part of the world and brings peace and understanding for people who have been adopted and do not know where their origins are.

Sycamore can listen deeply to and release guilt and regret over past actions. It can help dissolve the disappointment, sadness and despair that shape lives. It can heal tears of grief. People who have lost their way or feel like their life has spiralled out of control can find relief and healing with Sycamore.

The Sycamore can remind people who they are and what they are here for on a subconscious level. It brings an awareness of purpose, karma and particularly how it affects those around them. It helps us understand the point of view of others, without judgment. Our motivation becomes clear and true.

Five miles due south of the sacred site of Roslyn Chapel near

Edinburgh, Scotland, there is a low hill. Crowning this hill there is a grove of thirteen trees. The thirteenth tree is set off-centre and has been struck by lightning. All these trees are Sycamore. In the centre of the grove is the ruin of a 14th century chapel and it was here on Mount Lothian that William Wallace was knighted. These Sycamores were undoubtedly planted. The usual life span is about two hundred and fifty to three hundred years and this may be the second or even third planting. A sacred tree, it will protect any site. It is controversial that Sycamore is so often thought of as an incoming weed.

The Sycamore is one of the few trees that can thrive on the wet, windswept western islands.

Trunk

Here is a practice for you to set up working with your everyday senses with the tree. For Sycamore I am asking you to sniff the tree! Yes, smell it. Put your nostrils to its trunk and branches and inhale the scent. Ask that the Sycamore can heal your lungs of grief, your chest and back from guilt or your mind from confusion and despair. Breathe it deeply. You might begin to have visions of something coming off of you. Visualise the Sycamore helping to cleanse your soul and bring strength and clarity for your purpose.

Branches

Here are pathways you can take with the tree opening up whilst spending time with it or whilst accessing the realms behind this one in a journey.

Find yourself with the Sycamore or with a part of it you have been gifted. Feel an orb of light around you and set the intention that you take on nothing in this journey and are only available to meet the spirit of the Sycamore tree. Put your hands on the tree or tree part and imagine you go inside the tree. If you are holding just a twig imagine the rest of the tree in front of you.

Now ask to attune to the spirit of the tree and ask them to take you to the in-between worlds they reside in. What do you find here? Ask the spirit of the tree to show you its medicine. Ask to be shown how the tree communicates and how we humans can attune better to its energy and its ways. Ask if you can do something to support its role in life.

Leaves

This is a healing exercise you can access with the tree that works with the intention you bring to the book. Before you go into this healing exercise, read the intention that you brought to the book. You can read it out loud to the tree or you can hold this intention in your heart.

Lie under the Sycamore tree or put a twig or part of the tree on your chest. Take some breaths and let yourself feel this great tree energetically attuning to you and your whole self energetically attuning to it.

Now hold what feels significant about your intention for the book in your heart. Ask that the tree deeply listens to this. If you are buying beneath the tree, then with your eyes open, take in the full extent of the tree as you view it above you with its branches and the trunk. Allow yourself to feel the roots going beneath you too and searching into the earth. Take in the tree with your eyes and feel how as you touch it with your sight you are listening deeply to the Sycamore at the same time as it is listening to you.

If you have the twig on your chest then let your heart and senses feel into the twig and move into a journey as you have your eyes closed. Imagine yourself climbing and touching with your hands every part of the tree and then going into the earth to touch its roots. Listen with your whole being as you allow it to listen to what you hold in your heart.

After about fifteen minutes, come back to your everyday self and take some notes.

Seeds

Here you take the seeds from the tree to seed your own creativity through story. The seeds of the Sycamore are the classic helicopters. If you have some, you can hold one in your hands. It is Winter so it might be that you have a look on the internet for some photos of the two winged seed to inspire you and help you to tune in.

For this story, think about an area in your life that you feel divided at the moment. You can ask the Sycamore to show you what to look at in a journey, or you can go with your inspiration. It might be two parts of your personality don't work together easily. It might be that you have a choice to make and a fork in the road. It be that you are not getting along with someone or that you want to leave a part of your life behind to choose something else or that you are finding it difficult in a grieving journey to move on.

When you have found your area to look at, imagine you take one of the wings of the seed in your mouth and then let the other be in the air. Breathe in and out doing this. Notice what happens to your breath. It will be like drinking through a straw from another world into this one. Be open to visions. See what visions come. Notice what happens to your third eye. Notice how you feel the world around you turn into another land. Who is in this land? What are the colours like? Keep sucking on and drinking from the seed you imagine in your mouth. Take breaks to write down notes and then go back to the seed again. Who appears around you? What do they tell you? What do they show you? Can you hear any music?

When you have gone in deep enough and got some ideas and guidance, bring your ideas to paper to write a short story called 'The World I couldn't see'. See what flows.

Questions to complete

1. What is Sycamore to you?
2. What did Sycamore help you to see?
3. What did Sycamore listen to in you?
4. How do you feel different after your work with Sycamore?
5. How will you work with Sycamore in your work with others?

Now tune into Sycamore as you drum and thank it for its time with you and know that you can connect with it at any time. You are ready to work with a new tree.

Chapter 2

Beech

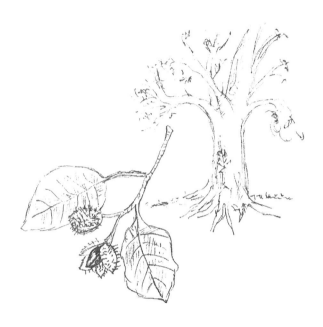

The Beech tree is esoterically connected with the planets Mercury and Saturn. It is known as a holder for the order in all of life and communicates this in its role on earth. Its natural habitat extends over a large part of Europe from southern Sweden to Northern Sicily. It requires a humid atmosphere and well-drained soil and can be sensitive to winter frost.

It usually grows on drier, free-draining soils, such as chalk, limestone and light loams. Beech woodland is shady. Its fallen leaves and mast husks prevent most woodland plants from growing. Only specialist shade tolerant plants can survive beneath a Beech canopy. Beech woodland makes an important habitat for many butterflies, particularly in open glades and along woodland rides. The foliage from this tree feeds the caterpillars of a number of moths. Mice, voles, squirrels and birds gorge on its seeds.

So, remember this structure below is the one you will work with for each tree. Right now, give yourself ten minutes to read through this chapter. I then ask you to spend five minutes quietly attuning or drumming or rattling to ask to connect with the tree in spirit. Feel out into the earth around you for any trees of this species on the land.

Working with Beech

First you need to find a Beech tree! If you can't reach one easily see if you can take a bit of a branch from a Beech you find. You can ask the tree if it is willing to give you a small twig or see if there is one fallen to the ground. You can also work with seeds or leaves or a bit of its bark. Any part of the tree is good. You will now be working through this material with the tree parts to really get to know this tree:

Roots: This is the lore and it gives you information on the qualities that the tree you are working with you is renowned for holding.

Trunk: Here is a practice for you to set up working with your everyday senses with the tree.

Branches: Here are pathways you can take with the tree opening up whilst spending time with it or whilst accessing the realms behind this one in a journey.

Leaves: This is a healing exercise you can access with the tree that works with the intention you bring to the book.

Seeds: Here you take the seeds from the tree to seed your own creativity through story.

Roots
Beech's Lore

Common Beech is a large, deciduous tree, native to southern

England and South Wales. Its scientific name is *Fagus sylvatica* and it is from the Fagaceae family. Beech can live for hundreds of years with coppiced stands living for more than a thousand years.

Mature trees grow to a height of more than forty metres and develop a huge domed crown. The bark is smooth, thin and grey, often with slight horizontal etchings. The reddish brown, torpedo-shaped leaf buds form on short stalks, and have a distinctive criss-cross pattern. The young leaves of the Beech tree are lime green with silky hairs, which become darker green and lose their hairs as they mature. They are four to nine centimetres long, stalked, oval and pointed at the tip, with a wavy edge.

Beech is monoecious, which means that both male and female flowers grow on the same tree. This is in April and May. The tassel-like male catkins hang from long stalks at the end of twigs, while female flowers grow in pairs, surrounded by a cup. The cup becomes woody once pollinated, and encloses one or two Beechnuts (known as Beech mast). Beech is wind pollinated. Triangular Beechnuts form in prickly four lobed seed cases. The wood of the Beech has a superb grain that finishes beautifully when polished.

Topically, Beech can be used for skin disorders. The tar from it was used in an old remedy for eczema and psoriasis and a poultice made from the leaves helped to heal scabs. The water collected from the hollows of ancient Beeches was thought to heal many skin complaints, and stuff your mattress with Beech leaves to speed up the healing process. Bark preparation was used to help reduce fever. Beechnuts have served as food for humans and animals. The essence of Beech can boost confidence and hope. A flower remedy from Beech enhances sympathy and tolerance

Beech is sacred to Obraash the Sun lord, whom the Elves call Alba. The Beech tree is a large and spreading tree bearing edible nuts. It was particularly valued by the ancient Celts – and the Elves – as a nut used to fodder animals, especially the sacred swine. Beech is the family of trees to which Oak belongs, thus is

Beech sometimes called Atarya Dwyrion, 'Grandfather of Oaks'. The name Beech relates to the Germanic word for book and tradition tells that Beech wood was used to make the first writing tablets for the runes. Hence, Beech is deeply associated with learning and lore, and with the divinatory power of the runes.

Like Greek Apollo, the Elvish Alba drives his sun-ship across the sky each day and passes to every world of manifestation, sources of light, beauty, and life. Apollo is also considered to be a spirit of youth, archery, and prophecy, the latter because of his conquest of the Pythian serpent at Delphi and subsequent assumption of the powers of the Delphic oracle. In Celtic tradition many gods are associated with the sun's light, among them Ogma Sunface, god of eloquence who created the ogham letters, and Oenghus mac Og, god of love and youth. The Elvish rune Sultan is the same as the Norse rune Sol, the solar rune. This word has also been interpreted to mean 'victory'.

Magical operations especially applicable to Beech include: spells of information, especially seeking old wisdom; invocation of ancient guardians or Ancestors; research into old writings and the runes; magic of the Summer Solstice, culmination of desires; magic of victory.

Trunk

Here is a practice for you to set up working with your everyday senses with the tree. For Beech, I am asking you to work with the sense of touch. Stand with Beech at your back or lean against it with your whole body. Press your palms into the bark of the trunk. Let your palms communicate love and appreciation for this tree being. Allow yourself to feel the energy of this tree through your hands and your body. You might also press the side of your face onto it. Stay like this for at least ten minutes. What does it feel like to have such a close physical encounter with this tree? How does it hold you? How does it feel to the touch? How do you feel being so close to it?

Imagine that by touching and being physically close to the Beech that you are able to receive a transmission through your body from the tree. Be available for your hands and your body to sense whatever it is that the Beech holds as its wisdom and information. Imagine that it can download from its form to your form through touch and proximity. Be open. Don't think about this. Just be open and see what this feels like. Wisdom is not an intellectual matter.

Take some time to let yourself absorb the experience and take some notes. Thank the Beech for being so available for you.

Branches

Here are pathways you can take with the tree opening up whilst spending time with it or whilst accessing the realms behind this one in a journey.

Find yourself with the Beech or with a part of it you have been gifted. Feel an orb of light around you and set the intention that you take on nothing in this journey and are only available to meet the spirit of the Beech tree. Put your hands on the tree or tree part and imagine you go inside the tree. If you are holding just a twig imagine the rest of the tree in front of you. Now ask to attune to the spirit of the tree and ask them to take you to the in-between worlds they reside in. What do you find here? Ask the spirit of the tree to show you its medicine. Ask to be shown how the tree communicates and how we humans can attune better to its energy and its ways. Ask if you can do something to support its role in life.

Leaves

This is a healing exercise you can access with the tree that works with the intention you bring to the book. Before you go into this healing exercise, read the intention that you brought to the book. You can read it out loud to the tree or you can hold this intention in your heart.

Sit beneath the Beech tree or put a twig or part of the tree on your chest. Pick up your drum or rattle and begin to make a steady beat or a steady shaking movement and open up to be able to drift more deeply into the imaginal realms.

Start to imagine or see yourself and your consciousness entering the Beech tree through a door that appears in its trunk. Meet the spirit of the Beech and ask the Beech spirit to take you to meet the ancient guardians and ancestors.

You may be taken into a world deep beneath the roots of the Beech. Or perhaps you will be taken up through the branches and out beyond the stars. When you arrive at the ancient guardians and ancestors, see what they have to tell you. Let the Beech spirit guide you and find out why the Beech is such an important connector to the ancient guardians and ancestors. Ask the Beech and these ancient spirits to bring a healing for you to help you to reconnect to your roots. Ask them for medicine and guidance to bring back into your life to nourish the intention that has brought you to the *Trees are our Letters* book. After about twenty to thirty minutes, come back to your everyday self and take some notes.

Seeds
Here you take the seeds from the tree to seed your own creativity through story. The seeds of Beech are inside little hats that hold the beechnuts. See if you can find some around the tree that have been burst open. If there are none to be found you can connect with the spirit form of these hats instead.

Place one of the broken open beechnut hats on the top or crown of your head. You can also do this exercise placing the hat on your palm. Allow yourself to feel yourself as the nut that came from this opened hat. You can feel the hat growing bigger to encase you and be at the point of letting you go. Feel the connection with the Beech tree and how you are born from it. Be aware of the wealth of power and lore that you are connected with. Be aware that you are of the tree that gives itself as the rune and the paper that will carry words of transmission. Feel your access to this lore and this wisdom. Feel yourself as this Beech sunlight held within a nut.

Now take a pen or an i-pad, laptop or phone and begin to write a story beginning with the words: 'I am light and this is my story. These are the words I have to bring to you today...' See what flows. Feel free to edit and change after you have brought the light through and also to change the first words given as guidelines here.

Questions to complete

1. What is Beech to you?
2. What did Beech help you to understand?
3. What did Beech open in you?
4. How do you feel different after your work with Beech?
5. How will you work with Beech in your work with others?

Now tune into Beech as you drum and thank it for its time with you and know that you can connect with it at any time. You are ready to work with a new tree.

Chapter 3

Cedar

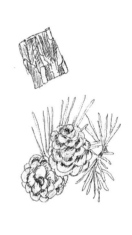

Cedar is a tree that has a few forms! I am including a most common to Britain and a more common to the US one for this book. The Cedar I am working with for the British tree is the Cedar Deodar, also known as the Himalayan Cedar. The one I am working with for the US tree is the white Cedar, also known as thuja occidentalis and the Tree of Life.

Cedar Deodar

Cedrus deodara, the deodar Cedar, Himalayan Cedar, or deodar is a species of Cedar native to the western Himalayas. It is an evergreen reaching forty to fifty metres tall, exceptionally sixty metres, with a trunk up to three metres in diameter. It has a conic crown with level branches and drooping branchlets.

The leaves are needle-like, mostly two and a half to five centimetres long, occasionally up to seven centimetres long, slender, borne singly on long shoots, and in dense clusters of twenty to thirty on short shoots; they vary from bright green to pale blue in colour. The female cones are barrel-shaped, seven to thirteen centimetres long and five to nine centimetres broad. They disintegrate when mature (in twelve months) to release the winged seeds that appear a bit like pips. The male cones are four to six centimetres long, and shed their pollen in the autumn.

White Cedar

Thuja occidentalis (Yellow Cedar/White Cedar/Eastern White Cedar/False white Cedar/Northern white-Cedar/ Swamp Cedar/ Eastern arborvitae) is also known as the tree of life.

Cedar holds the qualities of purification and protection. It also represents incorruptibility and eternal life. It has a strong association with overseeing the power of prayer. It is an old Jewish custom to burn Cedar wood to celebrate New year. With Cedar, we step into a time working with ideas around eternal life and the embodiment and living of our eternal spiritual nature.

So, remember this structure below is the one you will work with for each tree. Right now, give yourself ten minutes to read through this material. I then ask you to spend five minutes quietly attuning or drumming or rattling to ask to connect with the tree in spirit. Feel out into the earth around you for any trees of this species on the land.

Working with Cedar

First you need to find a Cedar tree! If you can't reach one easily see if you can take a bit of a branch from a Cedar that you find. You can ask the tree if it is willing to give you a small twig or see if there is one fallen to the ground. You can also work with seeds or leaves or a bit of its bark. Any part of the tree is good. You will now be working through this material with the tree parts to really get to know this tree:

> *Roots:* This is the lore and it gives you information on the qualities that the tree you are working with you is renowned for holding.
>
> *Trunk:* Here is a practice for you to set up working with your everyday senses with the tree.
>
> *Branches:* Here are pathways you can take with the tree opening up whilst spending time with it or whilst accessing the realms behind this one in a journey.
>
> *Leaves:* This is a healing exercise you can access with the tree that works with the intention you bring to the book.
>
> *Seeds:* Here you take the seeds from the tree to seed your own creativity through story.

Roots
Cedar's Lore
Cedar Deodar

The tree is native to the Himalayas. It was introduced to Europe in 1822 and to the United States nine years later. Cedar is suited to mountainous climates with winter precipitation. Most often it is found in the UK when planted in parks and gardens of large estates.

Cedar deodar has been revered for its spiritual significance for thousands of years. Its wood was used for the doors of sacred temples and burned in cleansing ceremonies for purification. The tree was thought to house important gods and to be an entrance to higher realms.

Among Hindus, as the etymology of deodar suggests, Cedar is worshiped as a divine tree. Deva, the first half of the Sanskrit term, means *divine, deity*, or *deus*. Daru, the second part, is cognate with (related to) the words *durum, druid, tree*, and *true*. How beautiful is that! It can translate to mean 'timber of the gods'.

Several Hindu legends refer to this tree. The nag temple would be built in the centre of a clump of Cedar trees. Forests full of Deodar or Devadāru trees were the favorite living place of ancient Indian sages and their families who were devoted to the Hindu god Shiva. To please Lord Shiva, the sages used to perform very difficult tapasya (meditation) practices in deodar forests. Also, the ancient Hindu epics and Shaivite texts regularly mention *Darukavana*, meaning a forest of deodars, as a sacred place.

The English word Cedar comes from the Hebrew 'qatar' meaning to smudge. Cedar wood was used in purification rituals and cleansing. Ancient Sumeria revered the Cedar over seven thousand years ago, calling it the World Tree, the abode of Ea, their chief god. The Bible has numerous references to the Cedar, including its use in the Ark of the Covenant.

Cedar's rot-resistant character also makes it an ideal wood for constructing the well-known houseboats of Srinagar, Kashmir. In Pakistan and India, during the British colonial period, deodar wood was used extensively for construction of barracks, public buildings, bridges, canals and railway cars. Despite its durability, it is not a strong timber, and its brittle nature makes it unsuitable for delicate work where strength is required, such as chair making.

The deodar is the national tree of Pakistan. Deodar is used in Ayurvedic medicine. The inner wood is used to make incense as it is aromatic. It is also distilled into essential oil. As insects avoid this tree, the essential oil is used as insect repellent on the feet of horses, cattle and camels. It also has anti-fungal properties and is used to protect spices during storage. The outer bark and stem are astringent.

Cedar oil is used in aromatherapy. It has a characteristic woody odour which may change somewhat in the course of drying out. The crude oils are often yellowish or darker in colour. Its applications cover soap perfumes, household sprays, floor polishes and insecticides and is also used in microscope work as a clearing oil.

White Cedar

White Cedar is native to Eastern Canada and Eastern United States. Unlike the closely related Western Red Cedar (Thuja plicata), Northern White Cedar is only a small or medium-sized tree, growing to a height of fifteen metres. The tree is often stunted or prostrate in less favourable locations.

The current oldest living Eastern White Cedar (found in Ontario overlooking the great lakes) is one thousand and sixty two years old, having germinated in 952. A dead Eastern White Cedar has been found whose age was estimated at one thousand eight hundred and ninety years old. These are the oldest living trees in Canada and Eastern North America and one reason for Cedar's name, Tree of Life. Another reason for this name is that it is extremely rot resistant and its wood lasts a long time. And then the clearer spiritual reason is that it holds the wheel of life and the pathways to infinity and eternity within it!

The bark is red-brown, furrowed and peels in narrow, longitudinal strips. The seed cones are slender, yellow-green, ripening to brown, nine to fourteen millimetres long and four to six millimetres broad, with six to eight overlapping scales. They contain about eight seeds each. The branches may take root if the tree falls.

Among trees, white Cedar is the supreme healer. White Cedar is very useful for treating people who turn to various coping mechanisms in order to deal with the difficulties of our present age. Excessive behaviours (drug addictions, overeating) as well as those who have been sucked into materialism and escapist behaviours all benefit from spending time with White Cedar. It provides people with a way reconnect with the spiritual and the divine. It is also used homoeopathically for those who feel dirty, have self-loathing, feel worthlessness or shame due to their own behaviour or due to something experienced or inflicted upon them. It helps reconnect people with confidence. This is because Eastern White Cedar is able to go into the unconscious and connect us deeply, rather than through surface issues.

Thuja is derived from the Ancient Greek *thuya*, which means, 'to sacrifice' or *thusia*, a burnt offering. Given the nature of the uses of Cedar as a smudge for protection and clearing, this connection is clear.

White Cedar is a tree with important uses in traditional Ojibwe culture. It is often referred to as "Grandmother Cedar". This tree is the subject of sacred legends and is considered a gift to humanity for its myriad uses. This includes crafts, construction (planks, canoes), and medicine. In the 19th century, Thuja occidentalis extract is used as an externally applied tincture or ointment for the treatment of warts, ringworm, and thrush. The Ojibwa made a soup from the inner bark of the soft twigs. Others have used the twigs to make teas to relieve constipation and headache. It is also used in cleansers, hair preps, insecticides and soaps. Cedar is one of the four plants of the Ojibwe medicine wheel, associated with the north.

White-Cedar foliage is rich in Vitamin C and is believed to be the cure of the scurvy of Jacques Cartier and his party in the winter of 1535–1536. Due to the presence of the neurotoxic compound thujone, internal use can be harmful if used for prolonged periods or while pregnant.

It is said that human souls can be contained within Cedar. When you smell the aroma of the Cedar tree or gaze upon it standing in the forest, remember that you are looking upon your ancestor.

Tradition holds that the wood of the Cedar tree holds powerful protective spirits. If you can, carry a small piece of Cedar wood in their medicine bags worn around the neck. Place it above the entrance to your house to protect it. A traditional drum would be made from Cedar wood. In some stories, people who are seeking long life are transformed into Cedar trees by medicine men or deities (often for making a foolish request).

Cedar is also told as a Creation and Transformation Agent. In one story, the Great Spirit took a pinch of Cedar from his pocket and it turned into the animals. In several stories from the Pacific Northwest, Cedar is carved into seals or fish and the carvings are transformed into real animals that are able to follow instructions of the one who carved them. The Inuit also describe carved figures and totem poles to help illustrate the history of their people.

Cedar is connected to the Element of Fire and the Sun. Cedar has a strong connection to fire; this is consistent between material in the Western esoteric traditions and the Native Lore. In a Tsimshian legend, "Walks All Over the Sky," the sky was dark until one of the Sky chief's children made a mask out of Cedar that was in the shape of a ring. He lit the mask on fire and then walked from east to west. When he slept after his journey each day, sparks flew from his mouth and these were the stars. So, in this way, Cedar is connected with the sun itself. In other legends, Coyote, a trickster, to create a torch, uses Cedar. This torch is usually attached to his tail and is used to light his path, often burning things on the way.

Cedar has a reputation as being cleansing and protective. A Cedar talking stick represents cleansing; likewise, Cedar is used extensively in ceremonial work in lodges and other ceremonies for purification. In a Hopi birth ritual, a newborn is repeatedly washed in Cedar tea and rubbed in cornmeal before being presented to the community. The Yuchi call the Cedar the 'great medicine'.

Trunk

Here is a practice for you to set up working with your everyday senses with the tree.

For Cedar you will be working with your sense of sight. You will sit or stand in front of the Cedar tree for about twenty minutes. Let yourself take in its form. Observe the patterned surface. Observe its relationship with the landscape and the air around it. Be really thorough at allowing yourself to greet the Cedar tree with your eyes. Admire and feel the great presence of this Great Spirit who has come into form. Allow yourself to acknowledge your own appearance as a great spirit come into form and observe your arms, body, legs, feet and your relationship with the landscape and the air around you. Take a good five minutes to get into this space.

Now stand or sit in the space you are in allowing yourself to take in the aura of the Cedar with your eyes. Make space to allow the vision of what goes beyond its physical dimension to come into sight. You can allow about ten minutes for this.

Now allow space for whatever goes beyond your physical dimension to come into sight. Allow about five minutes for this. Complete by bowing to the Cedar and thanking it for opening up the eyes of spirit in you. Take notes. You can return to this exercise later and keep practicing it to train your eyes to be open to the spiritual dimension.

Branches

Here are pathways you can take with the tree opening up whilst spending time with it or whilst accessing the realms behind this one in a journey.

Find yourself with the Cedar or with a part of it you have been gifted. Stand with your back to the tree if you are with the whole tree, or hold the twig or part of the tree you have been gifted and call the spirit of the Cedar tree to be behind you. Feel an orb of light around you and set the intention that you take on nothing in this journey and are only available to meet the spirit of the Cedar tree.

Feel yourself slip through the spirit of the Cedar tree so that you go to a place inside its mysteries. Here you find a grove of Cedar trees all about you. Ask the Cedar spirit to let you absorb and be purified by the power of the temple it provides for you.

Ask for a cleansing from the tree of any sense of worthlessness or shame that is blocking you from living the potential of your spiritual nature. Ask for guidance on an animal spirit who can come forward to support you to follow your own innate spiritual path of calling in your everyday life. Interview the animal spirit along with the Cedar spirit.

Thank the tree and its spirit for what it has helped you with and shown you. Now bring yourself fully back to presence in your own body. Feel yourself clearly take your form and step away from the tree or spirit tree and stamp your feet on the ground. Take some notes. Ask the Cedar for a piece of its branch to carve or draw the image of the animal spirit you connected with on. Take time to do this on a small piece. Carry this around with you.

Leaves

This is a healing exercise you can access with the tree that works with the intention you bring to the book. Before you go into this healing exercise, read the intention that you brought to the book. You can read it out loud to the tree or you can hold this intention in your heart.

Take a branch with Cedar leaves and hold the needles of the branch. Feel the vibration of the needles between your fingers and thumb. Allow yourself to open up and feel the air waves change and facilitate a flow. This might take a few minutes. Now make the decision to drift through the vibration you are connecting with. Ask the needles to transport you to the vibration of your destiny and your path in this lifetime according to the intention you have brought for this training. Be open to visions. Be beyond expectations. Just remain open. After about twenty minutes, come back to your everyday self and take some notes.

Seeds

Here you take the seeds from the tree to seed your own creativity through story.

The seeds of the Cedar are held within the female cones and open after about a year of maturation.

Hold a cone in your hands. Take some time to attune to it. Now lie down and place the cone on your forehead. If you don't have a cone available, then you can do this through calling in the spirit of the cone. You can imagine a seed being released by this cone onto your third eye. Let it go inside your third eye. Take it in and ask the seed to sprout a story for you in there.

Feel the seed take root. What is it placing its roots in? What is nourishing it? Can you feel the beginnings of story? What does story take as a form? What is the spiritual expression of story as a young shoot? What is the spiritual expression of story as a grown story? Where does story have to go to be comprehensible as a story? What does story have to grow into to be able to transmit the clear essence of story to you as a human? What does it feel like in your third eye? What colours do you see? Now take the seed of story out of your third eye and sprinkle it on your keys board of your laptop or onto your phone or laptop screen, or into a pen. Start to write. Title your piece: *The Story of Story.*

Do something to thank Cedar and its seed for the inspiration.

Questions to complete

1. What is Cedar to you?
2. What did Cedar help you to release, purify or heal?
3. What did Cedar do to your creativity?
4. How do you feel different after your work with Cedar?
5. How will you work with Cedar in your work with others?

Now tune into Cedar as you drum and thank it for its time with you and know that you can connect with it at any time. You are ready to work with a new tree.

Chapter 4

Poplar

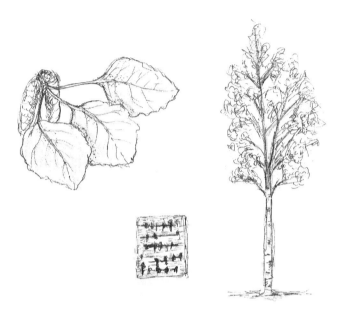

There are a few different types of Poplars. Amongst them are:

Balsam Poplar (Populus balsamifera)
Eastern Cottonwood *(Populus deltoides)*
Bigtooth Aspen (Populus grandidentata)
Black Poplar (Populus nigra)
European Aspen (Populus tremula)
Quaking Aspen (Populus tremuloides)
Black Cottonwood (Populus trichocarpa)

The Celtic name for Poplar is Eadha (pronounced: "Eh'uh"). Members of the willow family, Poplar trees are either male or female, with only the female producing the seeds. These are encased in white fluffy masses of hairs. Trees can regrow from the roots. Poplars are rapid growers and tolerant of a wide variety of growing conditions.

Poplar flowers appear in catkins that hang from tree branches in spring before the leaves emerge. Once the female flowers are wind-pollinated from male trees, seeds begin to form, maturing in late spring or early summer just after the leaves have grown out. Small round fruit capsules on the catkin split open, revealing small seeds surrounded by white cottony hairs. The wind catches the fluffy hairs and carries the seeds long distances from the parent tree.

The Poplar flourishes beside rivers, in marshes and in other watery areas. Its pith is star shaped and the upper leaves are green, the underside silver. The wood was used in the making of shields. Leaves move with the gentle breeze. It is commonly referred to as the talking, whispering and quivering tree.

The Anglo-Saxon rune poem seems to refer to the Poplar as being associated with the rune berkano. In Greek myth, Heracles wore a crown of Poplar leaves when he retrieved Cerberus from Hades, and the upper surface of the leaves was thus darkened from Hades' smoky fumes. Aspen crowns have been found in ancient burial mounds. It is thought they may have been included to allow the spirits of the deceased to return to be reborn.

In Christian lore, the quaking Poplar (aspen) was used to construct Christ's cross, and the leaves of the tree quiver when they remember this fact. The Poplar's ability to resist and to shield, its association with speech, language and the Winds indicates an ability to endure and conquer. So, you can see it is a very noble and sensitive tree.

At this stage of the book, we move a bit deeper into nature. The doors have opened for us and we are finding our way with the tree Queendom and Kingdom. Now the trees invite us to nestle in closer to the creative force of the communication systems they hold (and that we hold too when we realise it). With Poplar, we attune to the power of the muse. So, bear your aspen crown, and come inside!

Right now, give yourself ten minutes to read through this chapter. I then ask you to spend five minutes quietly attuning or drumming or rattling to ask to connect with the tree in spirit. Feel out into the earth around you for any trees of this species on the land.

Working with Poplar

First you need to find a Poplar tree! If you can't reach one easily see if you can take a bit of a branch from a Poplar that you find. You can ask the tree if it is willing to give you a small twig or see if there is one fallen to the ground. You can also work with seeds or leaves or a bit of its bark. Any part of the tree is good. You will now be working through this material with the tree parts to really get to know this tree:

Roots: This is the lore and it gives you information on the qualities that the tree you are working with you is renowned for holding.

Trunk: Here is a practice for you to set up working with your everyday senses with the tree.

Branches: Here are pathways you can take with the tree opening up whilst spending time with it or whilst accessing the realms behind this one in a journey.

Leaves: This is a healing exercise you can access with the tree that works with the intention you bring to the book.

Seeds: Here you take the seeds from the tree to seed your own creativity through story.

Roots
Poplar's Lore

The Poplar's distinctive canopy of round leaves with serrated edges and pale undersides, mounted on long, laterally flattened stalks gives the tree the unique appearance of shimmering or quivering in the wind. The aspen in particular have a delicacy so that they make a distinctive rustling, whispering sound. In many cultures and religions, the wind is associated with the voice of Spirit, and so in the boughs and leaves of the aspen the wind finds a distinctive voice to inspire those who would listen with patience and sensitivity. The movement of the wind through the canopy and the sun dappling through the leaves can have a mesmerising effect, encouraging a contemplative and meditative frame of mind. Like the hero and shaman who stand apart from the crowd, the Poplar's sparse distribution, often away from other trees, and its magical connotations has done much over the years to facilitate legends of people disappearing from under it into the land of Faerie.

Aspis, the aspen's Greek name, means shield. Amongst the Celts its lightweight wood was indeed favoured for making shields. These shields were more than mere physical barriers between warrior and enemy; they were imbued with additional magical, protective qualities to shield the bearer from psychic as well as physical harm. The magically protective nature of the 'shield tree' extended to the general population too and, like the rowan tree, was a popular choice of tree to plant close to a dwelling; buried treasures were also said to be protected by aspens.

In the Scottish Highlands the Poplar's Gaelic name is critheann (pronounced cree-an) as in Sron a critheann in Ardgower, (the Gaelic verb for tremble being crith). Here too the Poplar is considered a magical tree – an aspen leaf placed under the tongue would make the bearer more eloquent, traditionally a gift of the Faerie Queen. Several Highland folk taboos, including those against using the wood for fishing or agricultural implements, or in house construction, suggest that the aspen may have been considered a faerie tree on a par with the rowan tree.

Poplar wood is very lightweight when dried, becoming very buoyant and was therefore a popular choice for oars and paddles. Its lightness also made it useful for surgical splints and wagon bottoms. Its softness and lightness, though ideal for sculpting, are not suitable for use in building, though floorboards were sometimes made of aspen as a safety measure, as aspen wood does not burn easily. Poplar's shoots and leaves are popular with grazing animals, and hand gathered aspen leaves were fed to cattle when other food was scarce.

Poplar is known for its properties of encouraging abundance. Carry Poplar buds with you when seeking employment. Crush and add them to traditional money incense when you work on commission and need to attract more funds. The Poplar buds may also be added to divination blends, a great ingredient for psychics wishing to attract more business, as well as improving their powers.

Poplar is known as the 'Tree that Transcends Fear'. They symbolise the magic of joy, the aging of the year, resurrection and hope – and are connected to the Otherworld. Poplar can be called on for magic done for success, passage and transformation, Hope, rebirth, divinations, shielding, endurance, agility in speech and language, protection, and love – and as an aid in astral projection.

Poplar is used in protection charms of all kinds. Poplar is a good wood to burn in balefires and ritual fires since it offers protection. Carrying Poplar can help to overcome the urge to give way under the burden of worldly pressures, and aids in determination.

Siberian reindeer-hunting cultures carved small goddess statues of Poplar wood. Offerings were given to the figures with this prayer:

Help us to keep healthy!
Help us to hunt much game!

Poplar buds are also sometimes added to flying ointments and used in astral travel. A medieval recipe for a flying ointment called for Cinquefoil, Poplar leaves, soot and bat's blood obtained at the wake of the new moon.

The trembling leaves of the Poplar tree can be read to divine messages from the God and Goddess, and also from spirits that drift into woods. In the US, the Poplar is the sacred World Tree of the Lakota nation. For the sun dance ceremony, a Poplar is carefully cut and lowered, then is re-erected in the centre of the dance circle. While being carried, the Poplar must never touch the ground. Green branches, a buffalo skull and eagle feathers were used to decorate the Poplar for this ceremony.

A country name for the aspen-Poplar is the shiver tree. Because of this, both trees were formerly credited with the power to cure agues and fevers. A very old magical tradition held that ailments could most efficaciously be treated by something that resembled their effects; and since ague causes the patient to shake and tremble, he was likely to be healed by the shaking tree.

In Gaelic, the tree was called peble and pophuil. Poplar is generally a plant of Jupiter, Saturn and the Sun and is associated with the element of water. Its color is rufous (red) and the bird associated with Poplar is the Whistling Swan. The stones associated with Poplar are amber, citrine quartz, sapphire and swan fluorite.

Poplar trees are sacred to the Mesopotamian goddess Ua-Ildak. The Grass King of Grossvargula, who was seen as having fertilising powers, went on horseback wearing a pyramid of Poplar branches and a crown. He led a procession of young men about the town and was then stripped of his branches beneath the Silver Lindens of Sommerberg.

Poplar is said to be the tree of the Autumn Equinox and of old age. The Black Poplar was a funeral tree sacred to Hecate as death goddess, to Egeria, and to Mother Earth. Plato makes a reference to the use of black Poplar and silver fir as an aid in divination. The silver fir, stands for hope assured and the black Poplar for loss of hope. The Grove of Persephone in the Far West contained black Poplars and old willows.

In ancient Ireland, the coffin makers measuring rod was made of Poplar to remind the dead that this was not the end.

Poplar can be used as a tonic, chiefly used in treating fevers. The infusion has been found helpful in treating chronic diarrhoea. The sap collected from the buds can be used to make a healing ointment for bruises, swellings, and some skin diseases. Teas can be made from the Poplar buds and are useful in helping treat arthritis and rheumatism.

Trunk

Here is a practice for you to set up working with your everyday senses with the tree. For Poplar you will be working with your sense of hearing. Depending on the time of year when you are reading this, it could be that the leaves of the Poplar won't be through yet. But remember the tree has a special relationship with the wind and that it is the whole tree that responds to the air. So, stand close to the tree. See if you can have your back touching the trunk. Feel the vibration of the air element with the tree. You can place your ear to the tree too, but the idea is with this tree that you listen with your whole being.

Let your body be a sensitive instrument like your eardrum. Open up your body to feel the tree as it receives and transmits with the air. Feel what opens in you and the impressions that come to you as you do this. Stay like this for about twenty minutes. Take notes. You can return to this exercise later.

Branches

Here are pathways you can take with the tree opening up whilst spending time with it or whilst accessing the realms behind this one in a journey.

Find yourself with the Poplar or with a part of it you have

been gifted. You can take a drum or rattle with you, or gently tap on the bark of the tree to create a steady rhythm. Connect with the spirit of the Poplar tree and say hello. Now ask to be opened up to the muse. The muse might appear as a single spirit or it might appear as a group of guides who represent different aspects of the muse.

Ask the muse or the muses to do an attunement for you. They may do this by dismembering and remembering you in a journey (taking you to pieces and then building you back up again). Or perhaps they will sing to you or connect you with the communication networks through sound. Be open to anything here!

When the attunement is complete, thank the muse or the muses. Turn to the Poplar spirit. Ask for guidance about your path with the natural way of your creativity. Also ask for guidance about how to thrive in the world with enhanced creative flow and be protected from the discord that will naturally happen as you move at a heightened frequency form those around you. Ask the Poplar spirit to give you a protective shield and any other medicine to carry that will keep you calm and strong. Return to the everyday, draw the shield you were given and take some notes.

When you go back, draw the shield design on a separate piece of paper and place it on the back of your front or back door. Ask that it brings protection to all of your transitions.

Leaves

This is a healing exercise you can access with the tree that works with the intention you bring to the book. Before you go into this healing exercise, read the intention that you brought to the book. You can read it out loud to the tree or you can hold this intention in your heart.

Sit beneath or stand with the tree, or hold a twig from the tree across the palm of your hand. Attune to the protective and power to bring abundance and provision that this tree carries. Now connect with a part of yourself that feels insecure or worried. If you don't have a sense of this, then ask to be connected to something in your ancestral or descendant desired lines where there is a feeling of instability or worry. This may be a feeling of being overpowered, or a sense of poverty or hardship. Ask the Poplar tree spirit and the spirits of the wind, the muse or muses and the otherworld that the Poplar tree holds great affinity and friendship with to come through to surround this place in you or in your bloodlines.

You just need to wait at this point and allow everything to gather with you at this place. Feel the love and the great encouragement that moves towards you and what you are struggling with or care so deeply about. How does this feel to have so much support and tenderness coming through just for you?

Merge and feel your ancestors or descendants merging with the power of protection and support that is here for you now. Feel an empowerment happening and a welding with your true self being allowed. Ask to be shown visions of prosperity and calm. Ask to be shown this beautiful healing and supportive energy moving into the field of the intention you are holding for this book.

After about twenty minutes, come back to your everyday self and take some notes.

Seeds

Here you take the seeds from the tree to seed your own creativity through story. The seeds of the Poplar are housed in the round fruit capsules of the catkin. The fruit capsules split open to reveal small seeds surrounded by white cottony hairs. The wind will catch the fluffy hairs and carry the seeds long distances from the parent tree.

Take a fruit capsule from a catkin, if you can and hold it in your hand, or better still, see if you can find the fluffy hair with the seeds inside it. You can also imagine this if you don't have access to the catkin of the tree.

Now imagine yourself as one of these seeds being carried in the light fluffy hair. Feel yourself being drawn by the wind and all the spirits that work with the wind. Feel the wind as the muse facilitating your passage to a resting place where you will eventually take root.

Let some words flow to make the skeleton of a poem that describes your journey and the sensations as you are wrapped in the hair and as you feel the force of the wind and the spirits that work with the wind. Be very focused on feeling the power and the forces that are there with the wind and the spirits. What is it like surrendering to this? What is it like being so close to these forces of destiny and holders of rebirth and change? Give your poem an appropriate title.

Questions to complete

1. What is Poplar to you?
2. What did Poplar help you to open to?
3. What did Poplar do to your creativity?
4. How do you feel different after your work with Poplar?
5. How will you work with Poplar in your work with others?

Now tune into Poplar as you drum and thank it for its time with you and know that you can connect with it at any time. You are ready to work with a new tree.

Chapter 5

Magnolia

The Magnolia flower is a very old flower. There are fossils dating back twenty million years that show that the flower has been gracing Earth since the very beginning of time, so to say. This tree was 'discovered' by a French botanist, Charles Plumier, on the island of Martinique (France). Locally referred to as 'talauma', he gave the species the genus name Magnolia, after Pierre Magnol, another famous French botanist. After Plumier, it was William Sherard, an English botanist who began using the genus name Magnolia.

Magnolia grandiflora, commonly known as the southern Magnolia or Bull Bay, is a tree of the family Magnoliaceae, native to Europe and to the United States. Reaching twenty seven and a half metres in height, it is a large, striking evergreen tree, with large dark green leaves up to twenty centimetres long and twelve centimetres wide, and large, white, fragrant flowers up to thirty centimetres in diameter. Flowers have six to twelve petals with a waxy texture, emerging from the tips of twigs on mature trees in late spring.

Although endemic to the lowland subtropical forests on the Gulf and south Atlantic coastal plain, Magnolia grandiflora is widely cultivated in warmer areas around the world. The timber is hard and heavy, and has been used commercially to make furniture, pallets, and veneer. The Magnolia is a very tough, hard flower, unlike other delicate flowers. This is owing to the fact that it has had to adapt to changing climactic and geological conditions in order to survive, and it is precisely due to this feature that the flower represents endurance, eternity, and long life.

Right now, give yourself ten minutes to read through the below. You could then spend five minutes or so quietly attuning or drumming or rattling to ask to connect with the tree in spirit. Feel out into the earth around you for any trees of this species on the land.

Working with Magnolia

First you need to find a Magnolia tree! If you can't reach one easily see if you can take a bit of a branch from a Magnolia you find. You can ask the tree if it is willing to give you a small twig or see if there is one fallen to the ground. You can also work with seeds or leaves or a bit of its bark. Any part of the tree is good. You will now be working through this material with the tree parts to really get to know this tree:

Roots: This is the lore and it gives you information on the qualities that the tree you are working with you is renowned for holding.

Trunk: Here is a practice for you to set up working with your everyday senses with the tree.

Branches: Here are pathways you can take with the tree opening up whilst spending time with it or whilst accessing the realms behind this one in a journey.

Leaves: This is a healing exercise you can access with the tree that works with the intention you bring to the book.

Seeds: Here you take the seeds from the tree to seed your own creativity through story.

Roots
Magnolia's Lore

The botanical name of Magnolia is *Magnolia grandiflora*. It is associated with the element of earth and the astrological signs of Capricorn, Taurus and Virgo. Ruling planets are the Sun and Venus. Its gender is female.

Magnolia is an ancient genus of plant having evolved even before bees appeared on the timeline. Therefore, they were pollinated by beetles! The giant blossoms on this tree developed to encourage pollination by beetles first. Some fossilised specimens have been found to date back approximately twenty-million years! This tree has been known to survive ice ages, mountain range formations and continental drift and still rises regally among other flowering trees with some of the most magnificent foliage.

The Magnolia flower meaning is attached with the symbols of nobility, perseverance, and love of nature. Soft and subtle in colour yet strong in appearance, the flower is representative of the beauty encompassing femininity and gentleness. Often men prefer to gift their female partner the Magnolia flowers, as an appreciation of their beauty.

In China, the Jade orchid or *Magnolia denudata*, has been cultivated for thousands of years. The Magnolia flowers mean 'certainly' when they are used at the beginning of other sentiments along with other symbols. In China, Magnolia flowers are symbols of purity and nobility.

In America, the Magnolia flower is largely associated with the South. The Magnolia is the harbinger of the arrival of spring and is the official state flower of Mississippi and Louisiana. Mississippi has earned the nickname 'Magnolia State' due to the abundance of Magnolia flowering blossoms. In fact, Mississippi also uses the Magnolia as its state tree. The city of Houston, Texas is called the 'Magnolia City' due to the scores of Magnolia trees growing along the Buffalo Bayou.

During the Victorian times, the Magnolia flowers symbolized dignity, nobility, poise, and pride. The strength of its bloom is also symbolic of self-respect and self-esteem. Since these flowers represent durability, strength of character, and bearing, they are widely used in weddings. You can see what an ancient, rooted, strong and grounding tree this is! Magnolias are also associated with the life force and therefore can be sent over on the occasion of birth. Their flowers also represent a love of nature.

Various parts of this tree have found popular uses across the world. In traditional Chinese medicine (known as *Hou Po)*, the bark is used for regulating Qi (life-force) and resolving stagnation. It helps with coughing, vomiting and bloating. The dental community has also taken interest in the Magnolia bark extract because it interferes with the formation of bacterial plaque.

Magnolia seedpods resemble exotic-looking cones. Later in the summer and early in autumn, they spread open to reveal bright red berries. The tree comes to life with birds, squirrels and other wildlife that love these tasty fruits. Inside the fleshy red berries are the Magnolia seeds. Sometimes, when conditions are just right, you may find a Magnolia seedling growing under a Magnolia tree.

In ancient China where the plant was called *Yu-lan* (Jade Orchid), only the Emperor was entitled to own a Magnolia and he would occasionally give a root as a sign of imperial favour. The ancient Aztecs also knew of the Magnolia tree, naming it *Eloxochitl* or 'Flower with Green Husk'. One superstition tells that a blossom placed in the bedroom will kill anyone who sleeps there. In Japan the blossoms are used to wrap some foods and eaten. The fragrance of the blossoms is thought to possess aromatherapy qualities that help reduce anxiety. Native Americans were said to avoid sleeping under the tree when in bloom because of its strong scent. Dreaming of Magnolia symbolises beauty, grace and elegance. It can also represent a need to feel protected and safe, or to be recognised.

Wands made from Magnolia will help to encourage a regal but gentile demeanour. There is an almost hypnotic quality to this wood that is commanding but unhurried. It will help the practitioner to make wise decisions and develop patience and endurance. Magnolia will inspire a graceful and elegant application of will and encourage one to see the beauty of nature everywhere.

The Magnolias are an extremely attractive variety of flowers that are not easy to miss, given their large size. These fragrant blooms are most commonly associated with the colour white, though they come in a variety of other colours as well, including pink, mauve, peach, yellow, lavender, and purple. Interestingly, the flowers of the Magnolia tree do not have petals and sepals like other flowers; instead, they are composed of tepals that are leaf-like, petal structures. These tepals form around six to twelve cup-like structures.

Trunk

Here is a practice for you to set up working with your everyday senses with the tree. For Magnolia, I am asking you to taste the tree! You can choose to eat one of the flowers if they are in blossom, or take a branch or leaf and let it rest on your tongue. Ask the tree if this is ok of course before you do this. Feel the taste of it going into your system through your taste buds and your saliva. Ask the tree's spirit to communicate its properties with you through taste. What happens to your body? What happens to your sense of self? What happens to your heart and your mind? Be sensitive to how communicating intimately with this tree in this way has an effect on you.

Ask the Magnolia to strengthen you. Feel this strength

entering you and stimulating the strength within in. Ask the Magnolia to increase your sense of belonging with the earth. Let your sense of taste connect with this. You might begin to have visions of fortification or a clearer sense of self. Visualise the Magnolia helping to boost your worth and self-esteem.

Branches

Here are pathways you can take with the tree opening up whilst spending time with it or whilst accessing the realms behind this one in a journey.

Find yourself with the Magnolia or with a part of it you have been gifted. Feel an orb of light around you and set the intention that you take on nothing in this journey and are only available to meet the spirit of the Magnolia tree. Put your hands on the tree or tree part and imagine you go inside the tree. If you are holding just a twig, imagine the rest of the tree in front of you. Now ask to attune to the spirit of the tree and ask them to take you to the in-between worlds they reside in. What do you find here? Ask the spirit of the tree to show you its medicine. Ask to be shown how the tree communicates and how we humans can attune better to its energy and its ways. Ask if you can do something to support its role in life.

Leaves

This is a healing exercise you can access with the tree that works with the intention you bring to the book. Before you go into this healing exercise, read the intention that you brought to the book. You can read it out loud to the tree or you can hold this intention in your heart.

Stand, sit or lie under the Magnolia tree or put a twig or part of the tree on your chest. Take some breaths and let yourself feel this great tree energetically attuning to you and your whole self energetically attuning to it.

Imagine yourself as you stand, sit or lie with the Magnolia, or feel a selected offering from the Magnolia on your chest, going back through your time line to the time of your birth. Feel into yourself newly born and connect with your life force back then as well as the intention you are holding right now for the book. Ask the Magnolia tree to bring a blessing to your birth. Feel the energy of Magnolia going back with you to this time. Feel the ancient power of the Magnolia and its vibration with the different eons of time. Feel how the Magnolia brings permission for you to evolve in the way that is just right for you as it blesses your birth.

You may feel emotional as you feel this deep empathy for you to make your own choices and the strengthening of life force that comes from this gentle powerful being.

Feel this power moving into your intention for the book as well. Breathe this deep into your being in this time as if you are also the baby breathing at the beginning of your life.

After about fifteen minutes, come back to your everyday self and take some notes.

Seeds

Here you take the seeds from the tree to seed your own creativity through story. The seeds of the Magnolia are inside the fleshy red berries that materialise from the cones.

Have your recorder on your phone or other equipment switched on for this exercise. You can work with a cone holding the berries with the seeds inside, or work with your imagination. If you have access to the cone and seeds then put the seed or seeds on your belly button. If you don't, then call to the cone with the seeds inside to bring its spiritual presence to your belly button.

Take some time to attune. When you feel a connection, imagine the seeds taking you back through time to ancient times when the tree was pollinated by beetles. Ask to connect with the power of the ancient beetle. You can also call on the scarab beetle from Ancient Egyptian tradition.

Ask to be opened up to the ancient and divine knowledge

that is in the seed. Ask to be opened up to the wisdom of the beetle. Ask that your belly button connects with an umbilical cord that connects you right back to the original mothers. Spend some time really tuning into this and feeling the strength of this creative and nurturing lineage going back through time.

Now let some sounds and words through. Just let them flow. Feel the beetle and the Magnolia seeds opening a gateway of communication right back to the source of the grounded feminine wisdom and beauty. Feel the connection to the source of the muse.

When you are complete, let go of the attachment to all of the elements of this experience. Listen to the sounds you have made, or go straight into writing the words of a song that is a healing chant.

You can use this chant in your work to open up your creative flow and to bring healing and feminine power to a situation or to yourself.

Questions to complete

1.   What is Magnolia to you?
2.   What did Magnolia help you to open to?
3.   What did Magnolia connect you with and how did it affect your self-worth or power?
4.   Has anything changed in you after your work with Magnolia?
5.   How will you work with Magnolia in your work with others?

Now tune into Magnolia as you drum and thank it for its time with you and know that you can connect with it at any time. You are ready to work with a new tree.

Chapter 6

Cherry

Cherry tree's splendour is steeped in magic, mystery and mythology! Cherry is a dainty tree with a rich and vivid history. Throughout Japan, the Cherry, or 'Sakura' tree symbolises good fortune, new beginnings and revival. Folklore says that when the Sakura spirits release their incredible fragrance in springtime, the gift of beauty and elegance is to be truly celebrated! The Cherry blossoms bloom just once a year for a short time. It is because of the short window of the emergence of their pale, gentle beauty that Cherry is also a teacher of brevity. It calls us to love more transparently and in appreciation of the brief time we share together with our loved ones.

The word 'Cherry' derives from the French *cerise* and Spanish *cereza* which evolved from the Greek place name *Cerasus*. The name is also synonymous with the city of Giresun in Northern Turkey, from where cherries were first exported to Europe. The native habitat of the species from which the cultivated cherries came is believed to be western Asia and Eastern Europe from the Caspian Sea to the Balkans.

The indigenous range of the sweet Cherry extends through most of Europe, western Asia, and parts of Northern Africa, and the fruit has been consumed throughout its range since prehistoric times. A cultivated Cherry is recorded as having been brought to Rome by Lucius Licinius Lucullus from North Eastern Anatolia, also known as the Pontus region, in 72 BC.

The generic name for the species is *Prunus.* This is also the Latin word for a plum tree. It is a deciduous tree growing to fifteen to thirty two metres tall, with a trunk up to one and a half metres in diameter.

There is a type of Cherry tree called the Bird Cherry that has a bitter fruit, and in theory it should have the botanical name *Prunus avium, avis* being the Latin word for a bird. But the botanical name for the Bird Cherry is *Prunus padus,* which is also the Greek word for a wild Cherry tree. The name for the British native wild Cherry is *Prunus avium, avium* literally meaning in Latin 'of the birds'. Therein lies the clue. So, you can see that the native wild Cherry, commonly called a *gean* from *guigne,* the French word for the tree, is the ancestor of cultivated cherries.

Cherry tree has silver-grey bark, smooth in the young plants. With age, it becomes rough and covered with fissures. It has long and slender green leaves that are oval in shape and serrated on the edges. Cherry tree develops beautiful white flowers during the spring with flowers that are arranged in clusters. Insects are in charge for the pollination of Cherry blooms. Varieties of Cherry trees develop pink flowers and these are often grown for ornamental purposes. They do not produce fruit.

Botanically speaking, Cherry belongs to the group of stone fruit (drupe). It has red, dark red or almost black smooth skin.

Fleshy meat is moist and usually red or yellowish in colour. Single, hard seed is located in the middle of the fruit. One tree produces around seven thousand cherries per year. Birds love the sweet fruits and will eat them before they are ripe. So that is why the sweet-fruited wild Cherry is called *Prunus avium* and the bitter-fruited bird Cherry is called *Prunus padus*.

So, remember this structure below is the one you will work with for each tree. Right now, give yourself ten minutes to read through this chapter. I then ask you to spend five minutes quietly attuning or drumming or rattling to ask to connect with the tree in spirit. Feel out into the earth around you for any trees of this species on the land.

Working with Cherry

First you need to find a Cherry tree! If you can't reach one easily see if you can take a bit of a branch from a Cherry tree you find. You can ask the tree if it is willing to give you a small twig or see if there is one fallen to the ground. You can also work with seeds or leaves or a bit of its bark. Any part of the tree is good. You will now be working through this material with the tree parts to really get to know this tree:

Roots: This is the lore and it gives you information on the qualities that the tree you are working with you is renowned for holding.

Trunk: Here is a practice for you to set up working with your everyday senses with the tree.

Branches: Here are pathways you can take with the tree opening up whilst spending time with it or whilst accessing the realms behind this one in a journey.

Leaves: This is a healing exercise you can access with the tree that works with the intention you bring to the book.

Seeds: Here you take the seeds from the tree to seed your own creativity through story.

Roots
Cherry's Lore

There is archaeological evidence that our ancestors have eaten cherries since prehistoric times. Cherry stones have been found in Bronze Age settlements dating back to 2000BC.

It is said that cherries were introduced into England at Teynham, near Sittingbourne in Kent, by order of Henry VIII, who had tasted them in Flanders. Cherries arrived in North America early in the settlement of Brooklyn, New York when the region was under Dutch sovereignty. Some ten to twelve species are recognised in North America and a similar number in Europe. The greatest concentration of species is in Eastern Asia.

In modern Japan, the festival of Hanami is held every year to celebrate the coming of the Cherry blossom in spring; family, friends and loved-ones congregate amongst the Cherry trees to celebrate and reflect upon their happy lives together so far. 'Hanami' is an ancient Japanese tradition of viewing Cherry trees while they are in bloom. Japanese people track weather forecasts which determines the exact time of blossoming and they gather in large numbers in parks and temples to celebrate the beauty of these flowers when they finally appear.

In ancient mythology the fruit of the Cherry tree contains the elixir that gives the Gods their immortality! In Chinese lore it was believed that the magical Phoenix slept on a bed of Cherry blossom to bless it with ever-lasting life.

In old Buddhist stories, the Cherry is representative of fertility and femininity. According to legend, a holy Cherry tree supported the mother of Buddha as she gave birth. The symbol of the ruby-red Cherry is also popular in western culture and the gift of a Cherry tree is said to bring good fortune and future happiness to the days to come!

If you find a wild Cherry tree growing in a wood, look carefully at the leaves. If they are in shade, they grow large to intercept as much light as possible. If they are exposed to sunlight, they tend to be thicker to concentrate the light and stimulate photosynthesis.

Cherry tree flowers may lift the spirits but the greyish-brown bark of *Prunus padus* emits an acrid smell. This was unpleasant enough to persuade our ancestors to believe that by putting it at the door of a house it would ward off the plague. And perhaps it did! In the past, Cherry tree bark was used to make fabric dyes, ranging in colour from cream to tan, and a reddish-purple coloured dye was obtained from Cherry tree roots. The bark, leaves and seeds of Cherry trees contain chemicals called cyanogenic glycosides. If fresh leaves are chewed the chemicals can release hydrogen cyanide, a poison which can be lethal for children and animals. Even small doses can cause headaches, tightness in the throat and chest and muscle weakness. Despite this potentially fatal characteristic the some of the indigenous American cultures use Cherry leaves to make teas for the treatment of colds and coughs.

Cherry trees have played a part in medical lore for centuries. Resin leaks from the bark and was used by children as chewing gum. It was used as a treatment for coughs and dissolved in wine to treat gall and kidney stones. The perceived anti-inflammatory and anti-bacterial characteristics of sour cherries have been part of the remedy stock-in-trade of herbalists for centuries. Henry VIII was said to believe that the fruit relieved inflammation of the joints caused by gout. More recently several studies have discovered that tart cherries contain the natural sleep hormone melatonin, claimed to be useful as a remedy for insomnia and jet lag. Research has shown that the ruby-red fruit also contains antioxidants and this may significantly reduce risk factors for cardiovascular disease, diabetes and even cancer.

Cherry tree folklore is associated with the cuckoo. The bird is said to have to eat three good meals of cherries before it can stop cuckooing, and in Buckinghamshire there is a traditional children's rhyme that says:

'Cuckoo, Cherry tree,
Good bird tell me,
How many years before I die?

The answer was said to be the next number of cuckoo calls that the listener heard!

Trunk

Here is a practice for you to set up working with your everyday senses with the tree.

Stand facing the Cherry tree with your ear against its trunk. You are going to work with your sense of hearing. If you don't have access to the Cherry tree, then call in the spirit of the tree or hold a branch in your hand to attune to its energy.

Take some time to come into your own body and feel your heart beat and to steady your breathing. Come into the present.

Be aware of the time of year and the different sounds that there are in nature at this time of year. Filter all the other sounds to be background and focus attentively on listening for the sound of this tree. Spend about fifteen minutes listening. Be open to the vibration of the Cherry tree. Feel the vibration of the tree meeting the vibration of your whole body. You might find the sounds come from a different range to what you are used to. Be open to any kind of sounds, it might be like a humming, chanting, singing, tapping or whistling.

How does the activity of listening intently to this tree make you feel? What is your sense of this Cherry tree being and the way it communicates through the vibrations of sound? When you are complete, make some notes.

Branches

Here are pathways you can take with the tree opening up whilst spending time with it or whilst accessing the realms behind this one in a journey.

Find yourself with the Cherry or with a part of it you have been gifted. Feel an orb of light around you and set the intention that you take on nothing in this journey and are only available to meet the spirit of the Cherry tree. Put your hands on the tree or tree part and imagine you go inside the tree. If you are holding just a twig, imagine the rest of the tree in front of you. Now ask to attune to the spirit of the tree and ask them to take you to the in-between worlds they reside in. What do you find here? Ask the spirit of the tree to show you its medicine. Ask to be shown how the tree communicates and how we humans can attune better to its energy and its ways. Ask if you can do something to support its role in life.

Leaves

This is a healing exercise you can access with the tree that works with the intention you bring to the book. Before you go into this healing exercise, read the intention that you brought to the book. You can read it out loud to the tree or you can hold this intention in your heart.

Remember the lore about the ancestors working with Cherry for its acrid smell that would ward off the plague? Well, lie, stand or sit next to the Cherry tree. Or perhaps you would prefer to call in the Cherry tree from a different place. Come into the present moment. Now lift up a drum and being to make a beat for the next fifteen minutes or put on your headphones to listen to a drumming track.

In this healing exercise, call to you your ancestors and feel them behind you. Now call to the bark of the tree and its odour. Now call the Cherry blossoms and its odour too. Travel with the spirit of the Cherry and the odour of its bark. Feel the odour as a spirit medicine. Travel through your ancestral lines to intuitively visit any places in your ancestral past where there has been death by plague or death by an infectious or terminal illness. Ask the odour of the bark as a spirit medicine to separate your ancestors one by one from the attachment to this disease. Then ask the odour of the blossom as a spirit medicine if it will bless the souls of each person with sweet love and let each of your ancestors know how special they are to you.

In time, return to yourself and ask the spirit of the odour of the bark and the blossom to bring a protective cover for you against any infectious or otherwise diseases and to bring a blessing of sweet love to your heart.

If you have a particular illness or disease that you are currently holding a fear around and a part of your body that holds this fear then ask the spirit of the bark's medicine to visit this place in your body and clear out, like a broom made of the bark, any impression laid on yourself through your ancestral or fear banks of the spirit of this illness. Then ask the Cherry blossom to bless this part of your body with sweetness and courage to love.

When you have completed, take some notes. Thank the tree. Perhaps you could tie something discretely and loosely to the tree to honour the love and the strength of all of your ancestors you have visited in this journey. How do you feel now?

Seeds

Here you take the seeds from the tree to seed your own creativity through story. Remember this piece of lore: In ancient mythology the fruit of the Cherry tree contains the elixir that gives the Gods their immortality! In Chinese lore it was believed that the magical Phoenix slept on a bed of Cherry blossom to bless it with ever-lasting life.

Take a Cherry with a stone inside it. Lie down and place it on your body over the place of your beating heart. You can do this with a real Cherry or with a Cherry in the journeying worlds. Ask the seed of the Cherry, the stone to communicate with your heart in this mortal body the essence of your heart in an immortal life. Take some time to allow the stone to really connect with your heart. Feel how your heart strengthens and how the mortal and immortal come together. Allow this strength to travel through your own body. What does this immortal-self feel like? What is the immortal world? What is your knowing form this place? Who do you 'turn into' when you are your immortal self? What is the gift of your immortal self? If you were in a story, what character would you be? What would your mission be? Who would you communicate with? Where would you go? What are you in love with or care deeply about in this immortal role? What do you need to come back into this body and communicate about? When you have a real sense of empowerment from this experience and have a sense of all of this, sit up and move to your writing place.

Write a story about the character and what they love and care about and how they change something in this everyday world. You can write it a bit like the Jack and the Beanstalk story and have the Cherry tree as the climbing to the immortal self if you need a starting point.

Questions to complete

1. What is Cherry to you?
2. What did Cherry help you to understand?
3. What did Cherry show you about love?
4. Has anything changed in you after your work with Cherry?
5. How will you work with Cherry in your work with others?

Now tune into Cherry as you drum and thank it for its time with you and know that you can connect with it at any time. You are ready to work with a new tree.

Chapter 7

Elm

Elms are deciduous and semi-deciduous trees from the plant family Ulmaceae. The genus first appeared in the Miocene age about twenty million years ago, originating in what is now central Asia. These trees spread over most of the Northern Hemisphere, inhabiting the temperate regions of North America and Eurasia. Now they range southward across the Equator into Indonesia. The tree is known as the tree of death.

Elm, English heartwood, is light to medium reddish brown. Its scientific name is Ulmus procera. Mature trees grow to thirty metres high and can live for more than one hundred years. The bark is grey brown, rough and fissured, often with suckers growing from the base of the trunk. The twigs are finely hairy. Buds are oval, pointed and hairy. Leaves are four to six centimetres in length. They are round to oval, toothed with a rough, hairy surface. They have a characteristic asymmetrical base and taper to a sudden point at the top.

English Elms are hermaphrodites, meaning both male and female reproductive parts are contained within the same flower. Flowers are dark pink to red and hang in tassels, appearing in February and March. Once pollinated by wind, the flowers develop into tiny winged fruits, known as samaras. These are dispersed by wind. Elms have distinctly asymmetric leaf bases. Leaves are rough to the touch on the top surface.

Wych Elm is more found in Scotland, hence its second name Scots Elm. The Scot Elm has slightly larger leaves. Both trees are native to the UK. American Elm is also known as Soft Elm, Water Elm. Its scientific name is Ulmus Americana. Its distribution is in Eastern to Midwest United States. It grows twenty to thirty metres in height.

Right now, give yourself ten minutes to read through this chapter. I then ask you to spend five minutes quietly attuning or drumming or rattling to ask to connect with the tree in spirit. Feel out into the earth around you for any trees of this species on the land.

Working with Elm

First you need to find an Elm tree! If you can't reach one easily see if you can take a bit of a branch from an Elm tree you find. You can ask the tree if it is willing to give you a small twig or see if there is one fallen to the ground. You can also work with seeds or leaves or a bit of its bark. Any part of the tree is good. You will now be working through this material with the tree parts to really get to know this tree:

Roots: This is the lore and it gives you information on the qualities that the tree you are working with you is renowned for holding.

Trunk: Here is a practice for you to set up working with your everyday senses with the tree.

Branches: Here are pathways you can take with the tree opening up whilst spending time with it or whilst accessing the realms behind this one in a journey.

Leaves: This is a healing exercise you can access with the tree that works with the intention you bring to the book.

Seeds: Here you take the seeds from the tree to seed your own creativity through story.

Roots
Elm's Lore

In Greek mythology, when Orpheus picked up his harp and played a love song to his rescued wife Eurydice from the Underworld (by enchanting everyone there with his harp music) on this spot the first Elm grove was said to have sprung up. In Celtic mythology Elm trees were also associated with the Underworld. They had a special affinity with elves the guardians of the burial mounds who would accompany the dead to the Underworld.

Elm trees in can grow to become some of the tallest and largest native trees. They have names like the Tenor, Bass and Alto Elms on Humberside, or the Dancing Elms of Devon. These were the trees around which May Day dances were held. They are used in hedges, and their stature made them good landmarks and boundary markers. Travelling preachers and judges would often pronounce from beneath them.

The Elm's wood bends well. The 'wych' in Wych Elm refers to its wood being pliant. It's not a good building wood but it withstands wet conditions well, making it a popular choice for the building of boat and barge hulls, bridge foundations, and cartwheels. Hollowed-out Elm was used to make urban water pipes before the introduction of metal ones. Its pliancy was also put to use in a variety of ways. In Scotland the stick used to play shinty is called a caman. It can be made from a variety of woods, with Elm being a popular choice as it often has a natural bend already in the wood. It can be easily be heated, bent and set to the required shape. Mediaeval Welsh archers made their long bows from Elm wood.

Elm's mythology is bound up with death and the transition into the Underworld and it is also a tree used to make weapons for death. Its wood was also traditionally used to make coffins, though the wood's durability underground may also play a part in this choice. People who knew Elms well were reminded of their own mortality when remembering the Elm's reputation for dropping large boughs without warning on otherwise still days. 'Elm hateth man, and waiteth' is an old saying. Elms are one of the favourite trees of rooks. They love to nest in their branches.

Indigenous American herbalists use Slippery Elm bark to wrap wounds. It was dried and powdered and then made into a paste by adding water then applied to injuries to flesh and bone. The tea of the bark, root and leaf was taken to speed bone healing. The powdered bark can be mixed with water to make a jelly that helps urinary and bowel problems, sore throats, scurvy and diarrhoea, and which can be eaten as a source of calcium for those allergic to cow's milk.

Slippery Elm poultices are effective for ulcers, tumours, swellings, gunshot wounds, chilblains, and can be placed on the abdomen to draw out fever. Injections of Slippery Elm tea are helpful for dysentery and haemorrhoids. The Iroquois made canoes from Elm as well as sleeping platforms and casks for shelled corn. The Potawatomi used Slippery Elm to poultice inflamed eyes, boils and splinters. Huron women made Elm vessels of various sizes that could hold up to one hundred gallons of liquid. The largest ones were made to hold maple sap. How helpful is Elm!

The Delaware used Slippery Elm to make a paste to keep canoes tight and the Meskwaki used Elm bark to cover their houses. The root of Slippery Elm can be boiled to make a tea that is said to ease childbirth when taken for a few months before delivery.

The Penobscot used a tea of White Elm bark for bleeding from the lungs. The Mohegan used it for coughs and colds and the Seneca made bark kettles of Elm. The Mohawk twisted Elm bark to make harnesses for sledges.

Elms were important fodder trees for farmers of the Neolithic. The shoots and leaves of Elm were once used to feed domestic stocks when other food was scarce or unavailable. The barks of both Elm trees were used to weave mats, footwear, baskets and wicker. Elm wood was an important material for bows. The Indo-European root word for Elm was most probably "wyg" from which came the Kurdish "viz", the Low German "wike" and the English "wych" from which the words ligature, binding, withy (for weaving), to bend, and to weave were later developed in several modern languages.

In Gaelic it is known as 'leven', as in Loch Leven in Kinross, and was valued for its roles in the dyeing of wool. Intermittent colours in woollen could be introduced by way of an early form of tie-dyeing. Twine made from the inner bark of the Elm was tied tightly at regular intervals, to form 'hanks' of the yarn. This would stop a dye from reaching the wool. A yellow dye could also be derived from the Elm.

Trunk

Here is a practice for you to set up working with your everyday senses with the tree.

Stand facing the Elm tree with your mouth close to its trunk. You are going to work with your voice. If you don't have access to the Elm tree, then call in the spirit of the tree or hold a branch in your hand to attune to its energy.

Take some time to come into your own body and feel your heart beat and to steady your breathing. Come into the present. When you feel attuned to being present in your own self and feel attuned to the Elm tree, open up to making some sounds. Let the sound flow freely as a response to the Elm tree. Notice the tone or the strength of your voice. As you are singing, humming, toning or chanting, be aware of your throat, your voice box and then your wind pipe and lungs. Continue to attune to the Elm. Feel how the effort of the vibration you make with sound moves through your whole body. Be aware of your lungs and your voice box. Feel yourself as an instrument.

Be open to the vibration of Elm tree. Feel the vibration of the tree meeting the vibration of your whole body and being. Be aware of the trunk and the branches of the Elm and then move to an awareness of its roots. Feel how it connects deep into the earth and into the underworlds. Hold the intention that as you make sounds, your sounds are opening up the underworld to you. Be in this space for about ten minutes.

When you come out of the exercise sit and ground for a while and then make some notes about your experience.

Branches

Here are pathways you can take with the tree opening up whilst spending time with it or whilst accessing the realms behind this one in a journey.

Find yourself with the Elm or with a part of it you have been gifted. Feel an orb of light around you and set the intention that you take on nothing in this journey and are only available to meet the spirit of the Elm tree. Put your hands on the tree or tree part and imagine you go inside the tree. If you are holding just a twig, imagine the rest of the tree in front of you. Now ask to attune to the spirit of the tree and ask them to take you to the in-between worlds they reside in. What do you find here? Ask the spirit of the tree to show you its medicine. Ask to be shown how the tree communicates and how we humans can attune better to its energy and its ways. Ask if you can do something to support its role in life.

Leaves

This is a healing exercise you can access with the tree that works with the intention you bring to the book. Before you go into this healing exercise, read the intention that you brought to the book. You can read it out loud to the tree or you can hold this intention in your heart.

Sit or stand with the tree in everyday time or call in the spirit of the tree. Let yourself acclimatize to it. Feel an orb of light around you that will keep you clear and not available to take anything but pure healing energy on. Remember how in Lore, it was said that Elm has a connection with the elves and the underworld? Now put out the intention to open to the frequency of the elves. Take your time. Be ready for a subtle vibration to begin with. I recommend that you stay in this space in total for at least twenty minutes.

After a couple of minutes, let the elves know that you are available to receiving a transmission from them. Feel the Elm tree anchoring you with the earth and then let the light web (or however you experience it) that the elves work with transmit to you and energise, balance, attune or clear you – whatever you are naturally ready for at this time. You might perceive movement or you might see visuals. You may feel revitalised, blasted or opened. Keep grounding yourself with the Elm tree and asking it to hold space for you.

After twenty minutes, bring yourself back. Spend some time looking around you and connecting with the landscape around you with your sight and your felt senses. How is the world now? Make some notes.

Seeds

Here you take the seeds from the tree to seed your own creativity through story. Elm samaras are papery pockets of green or sometimes red in which the seeds are stored. They can be eaten. For the story work find a photo of the samaras. Or if it is the time of year for seeding then find some samara pockets and hold them in your hand.

Now lie down. You are going to imagine that you are a samara connecting to and a part of the wider Elm and that your consciousness is the seed. Can you connect with the protective nature of yourself as a pocket or a bed for the consciousness? Feel your own body as a pocket or a bed for your consciousness.

Open up to the juiciness of this bed and the life that it is guardian of. Feel how it protects you as a consciousness. Now start to become conscious of all of the other seeds in pockets all around you on the Elm tree, and in turn with all the other seeds in pockets as humans who are here in this world with you. Feel the power of a wider consciousness. Feel a clearing and an opening happen so that anything that is bringing in fear or danger for connection is washed away by the power of the wider and greater consciousness.

Go deeper into our own consciousness as a seed and at the same time, feel yourself pulled by the current of the wider consciousness to what you and everyone as samara of the Elm and of the human race are truly connected with. Find yourself pulled to the underworld.

Let yourself be taken on a journey to the underworld and to where your consciousness truly resides. Feel the safe bed of the samara of the Elm and of your body all around you. Feel how much more real it feels in this place as a truth for what really is important and true for you. See what you see and what you hear and are shown. Take some time to come back. When you return, write up your experience as a story or a poem. You can start your writing with the line: *One day I reached out to the life beyond this one...* or similar words.

Questions to complete

1. What is Elm to you?
2. Where did Elm take you?
3. What is different about you after your time with Elm?
4. What is Elm's role here in this realm?
5. How will you work with Elm in your work with others?

Now tune into Elm as you drum and thank it for its time with you and know that you can connect with it at any time. You are ready to work with a new tree.

Chapter 8

Horse Chestnut

Horse Chestnut's scientific name is *Aesculus hippocastanum.* Carl Linnaeus named this genus and the word is derived from the Roman word for an edible corn. It is not native to the British Isles. It is believed to have originated in the Balkan region of Eastern Europe and have travelled to the UK via Turkey. In the US this tree is also known as the buckeye. It is known as the conker tree in Britain owing to its relation with the conker game that is played with the seeds also known as conkers (the strongest conker is the conqueror). Horse Chestnuts are in an entirely different botanical family from sweet chestnut tree, *Castanea vesca*. Horse Chestnuts exist as both a tree and a shrub, and are found in all temperate regions of Europe, Asia and North America. It thrives on any soil type as long as it is well drained.

There are fifteen recognized species of Horse Chestnut. The leaf stalks leave a scar on the twig when they fall, which resembles an inverted horseshoe with nail holes. This association with horses could explain why conkers used to be ground up and fed to horses to relieve them of coughs, and could be the origin of the tree's name.

Mature Horse Chestnut trees grow to a height of around forty metres, and can live for up to three hundred years. The bark is smooth and pink-grey when young. It darkens and develops scaly plates with age. Twigs are hairless. Buds are oval, dark red, shiny and sticky.

The leaves comprise of five to seven pointed, toothed leaflets spreading out from a central stem. Flowers appear in May and the individual flowers have four or five fringed petals. These are white with a pink flush at the base. Once pollinated by insects, the flower develops into a glossy red-brown conker inside a spiky green husk, which falls in autumn. The seeds are the conkers. They are surrounded by a spiky green case. In the winter Horse Chestnut can be recognised by its twigs having large sticky red buds.

So, remember this structure below is the one you will work with for each tree. Right now, give yourself ten minutes to read through this chapter. I then ask you to spend five minutes quietly attuning or drumming or rattling to ask to connect with the tree in spirit. Feel out into the earth around you for any trees of this species on the land.

At the end of the days, you will gently sign yourself out and thank the tree in the same way.

Working with Horse Chestnut

First you need to find a Horse Chestnut tree! If you can't reach one easily see if you can take a bit of a branch from a Horse Chesnut tree you find. You can ask the tree if it is willing to give you a small twig or see if there is one fallen to the ground. You can also work with seeds or leaves or a bit of its bark. Any part of the tree is good. You will now be working through this material with the tree parts to really get to know this tree:

>*Roots:* This is the lore and it gives you information on the qualities that the tree you are working with you is renowned for holding.
>
>*Trunk:* Here is a practice for you to set up working with your everyday senses with the tree.
>
>*Branches:* Here are pathways you can take with the tree opening up whilst spending time with it or whilst accessing the realms behind this one in a journey.
>
>*Leaves:* This is a healing exercise you can access with the tree that works with the intention you bring to the book.
>
>*Seeds:* Here you take the seeds from the tree to seed your own creativity through story.

Roots
Horse Chestnut's Lore

The lovely Horse Chestnut tree is traditionally known as a friend for all generations. It is both a wise old grandfather and a playful companion for the children. It provides shelter and stability and tends to meet us in the middle world as an equal. It is renowned for its ability to bring peace and grounding and draw our minds and emotions into focus in the everyday.

Horse Chestnuts in the house are said to keep away spiders and in drawers, moths. The common name of the Horse Chestnut is believed to have been derived from the traditional custom among the Turkish to feed nuts to their horses with a view to provide the animals with an antidote to flatulence.

The seed, bark, flower, and leaves are all used to make medicine. The tree can help people who feel very dejected, depressed and are touchy and can increase the ability to concentrate. It can also support bad temperedness. The Horse

Chestnut can also ease worry, especially toward the wellbeing of others. It helps to build boundaries around being overly sympathetic with others, and taking on the emotions of others. It can ground people and ease obsessive mind activity. Horse Chestnut contains significant amounts of a poison called esculin and can cause death if eaten raw.

Horse Chestnut seeds and leaves are used for treating varicose veins, haemorrhoids and swollen veins. Horse Chestnut seed is used to treat diarrhoea, fever and enlarged prostrate. Horse Chestnut seeds can be processed so that the active chemicals are separated out and concentrated. The resulting "extract" is used for treating blood circulation problems. Its leaf is also used for eczema, menstrual pain, soft tissue swelling from bone fracture, sprains, cough, arthritis and joint pains. Horse Chestnut branch bark is used for dysentery and malaria. Some people apply Horse Chestnut branch bark to the skin to help heal lupus and skin ulcers. Here are some sayings about the Horse Chestnut or conker:

Carry a conker (conker) in your pocket to get money.
The person who carries a conker in the pocket never becomes sick.
The person who carries a conker in the pocket never suffers from backache.
A conker carried in your pocket or the band of your hat prevents headache.

As a treatment for piles, a conker is carried in the pocket (usually the left), or one in each pocket, or one pinned to the underclothes, or one round the neck, or one rolled in the top of each stocking. Conkers used for curing rheumatism should always be carried in pairs. This also makes you lucky at the same time. If you carry three conkers in a sack next to your skin, it is said that they will be good for rheumatism. If the conkers dry up when you are wearing them, then they are doing you good. However, if they don't dry all up, they are doing you no good.

Trunk

Here is a practice for you to set up working with your everyday senses with the tree. Stand facing the Horse Chestnut tree and press your body to its trunk. You are going to work with grounding.

If you don't have access to the Horse Chestnut tree, then call in the spirit of the tree or hold a branch in your hand to attune to its energy. As with all the trees, take some time to come into your own body and feel your heart beat and to steady your breathing. Come into the present. Feel the bark and the trunk of the tree (or the branch) with your hands. Let the palms of your hands be sensitized to the texture and feel the energy of the tree. Feel your hands connecting to the tree as if you were dancing with the tree or holding hands with it. Now, simply feel the tree as a friend.

See what your new friend the Horse Chestnut tree has to offer you or be for you. Notice your breathing and your sense of being in your body as you spend the next ten minutes simply being available to the friendship of this tree through holding hands or dancing with it. When you come out of the exercise sit and ground for a while and then make some notes about your experience.

Branches

Here are pathways you can take with the tree opening up whilst spending time with it or whilst accessing the realms behind this one in a journey.

Find yourself with the Horse Chestnut or with a part of it you have been gifted. Feel an orb of light around you and set the intention that you take on nothing in this journey and are only available to meet the spirit of the Horse Chestnut tree. Put your hands on the tree or tree part and imagine you go inside the tree. If you are holding just a twig, imagine the rest of the tree in front of you. Now ask to attune to the spirit of the tree and ask them to take you to the in-between worlds they reside in. What do you find here? Ask the spirit of the tree to show you its medicine. Ask to be shown how the tree communicates and how we humans can attune better to its energy and its ways. Ask if you can do something to support its role in life.

Leaves

This is a healing exercise you can access with the tree that works with the intention you bring to the book. Before you go into this healing exercise, read the intention that you brought to the book. You can read it out loud to the tree or you can hold this intention in your heart.

Sit or stand with the tree in everyday time or call in the spirit of the tree. Let yourself acclimatize to it. Feel an orb of light around you that will keep you clear and not available to take anything but pure healing energy on.

Now connect with the leaves of the tree. If the tree is in leaf, then you can hold one in your hand. If not, imagine the leaves. Feel the five or seven fingers of the leaf reaching out to the world in its simple and direct way. Ask that you can match the reaching out of the leaf in your own simple and direct way. Feel yourself attuning to the spirit of the Horse Chestnut tree and hold your own hands open, palms out to feel the world. Ask the Horse Chestnut tree and its direct and open character to take from you anything that is disabling your ability to be yourself. Feel this as a kind of earthing activity. You might be aware of other beings working with the Horse Chestnut.

Sense what it is like to have the palms of your hands open with fingers and thumbs stretched to be available to meet with the earth and all who live here. Sense the tree as a friend again. Then begin to open up to the idea of connecting with everything else that is a friend to you in the world. Join with the forces of the tree to connect with the great network of befriending that is out there. Feel the enriching of your world as you do this. Now feel the befriending coming into the spirit of what it is you are holding for your intention for the book. Feel the support of a fellowship coming in especially for you and the dream and the vision you are holding. Let your palms and hands feel the power of this as a reality.

After twenty minutes, bring yourself back. Spend some time looking around you and feeling the lay of the land. How is the world now? Make some notes.

Seeds

Here you take the seeds from the tree to seed your own creativity through story. Take a conker from the Horse Chestnut tree. If you don't have access to a conker at this time, then connect energetically with this seed of the tree.

Lie down and place the conker as a physical form or as an energetic form between your legs at the base of your root chakra. Ask it to connect your roots with the root system of the Horse Chestnut trees and to tap you into the fellowship of these trees. Imagine yourself, your bloodlines and the veins in your body flowing with the root systems and the communication systems between the Horse Chestnut trees. Feel yourself rooting and grounding with the simple purpose of being here and befriending.

Now visualize yourself entering an important meeting place that is a Headquarters for the spirit of these trees to meet and discuss the balance and the holding of wellbeing for all. Let yourself be a scribe at their meeting. What do they talk about? What do they say? Let their words of encouragement and belief flow into your veins as you sit with the seed beneath your root chakra. Feel it bringing deep healing and strengthening to your arteries, veins and all your vascular structures. Feel the relief of being a part of a communication system of caring and support.

Take some time to come back. When you return, write a story or a poem called 'What I heard the trees say'.

Questions to complete

1. What is Horse Chestnut to you?
2. What did Horse Chestnut connect you with?
3. What is different about you after your time with Horse Chestnut?
4. What is Horse Chestnut's role here in this realm?
5. How will you work with Horse Chestnut in your work with others?

Now tune into Horse Chestnut as you drum and thank it for its time with you and know that you can connect with it at any time. You are ready to work with a new tree.

Chapter 9

Hornbeam

The Latin name for Hornbeam is *Carpinus betulus*. It is native to Western Asia and Central, Eastern, and Southern Europe, including Southern England. It is a deciduous tree. It requires a warm climate for good growth, and grows at elevations of up to six hundred metres. It grows in mixed stands with Oak, sometimes Beech, and is a common tree in scree forests. There are about thirty to forty species that live in temperate regions throughout the Northern hemisphere. In folk medicine a tonic made from Hornbeam helped to relieve tiredness and exhaustion. Hornbeam was also known as Yoke Elm. Horn means tough, hard wood and beam is the old English word for tree from the German, baum. American Hornbeam is also occasionally known as blue-Beech, ironwood, or musclewood. It is known as *Carpinus caroliniana*. It is a shade-loving tree native to the Eastern half of North America. Hornbeams can live to be three hundred years old.

The tree has pale silvery-grey bark. The leaves are oval with distinct double-toothed serrated edges. Hornbeam produces flowers of catkins of approximately three to four and a half centimetres in April or May. After pollination by wind, female catkins develop into papery, green winged fruits, known as samaras. It is a monoecious tree, meaning male and female catkins are found on the same tree. The fruit is a small seven to eight millimetre long nut, partially surrounded by a three-pointed leafy involucre three to four centimetres long. It matures in autumn.

It is one of the strongest of the hardwood trees. The tree can grow well in most places but has a preference for low-lying rich soils or clay and is shade-tolerant. It can be coppiced or pollarded.

Hornbeam is known as a bringer of confidence. It encourages us to remain optimistic even in the face of adversity. This is a time of knowing and trusting in the strength and integrity of our heart. By doing this we gain the confidence in ourselves to pursue our dreams. We must make the effort to change and begin moving in the direction that is calling us.

Right now, give yourself ten minutes to read through this chapter. I then ask you to spend five minutes quietly attuning or drumming or rattling to ask to connect with the tree in spirit. Feel out into the earth around you for any trees of this species on the land.

At the end of this time you will gently sign yourself out and thank the tree in the same way.

Working with Hornbeam

First you need to find a Hornbeam tree! If you can't reach one easily see if you can take a bit of a branch from a Hornbeam that you find. You can ask the tree if it is willing to give you a small twig or see if there is one fallen to the ground. You can also work with seeds or leaves or a bit of its bark. Any part of the tree is good. You will now be working through this material with the tree parts to really get to know this tree:

> *Roots:* This is the lore and it gives you information on the qualities that the tree you are working with you is renowned for holding.
>
> *Trunk:* Here is a practice for you to set up working with your everyday senses with the tree.
>
> *Branches:* Here are pathways you can take with the tree opening up whilst spending time with it or whilst accessing the realms behind this one in a journey.
>
> *Leaves:* This is a healing exercise you can access with the tree that works with the intention you bring to the book.
>
> *Seeds:* Here you take the seeds from the tree to seed your own creativity through story.

Roots
Hornbeam's Lore

Hornbeam has extremely hard close-grained wood that is good for redwood and producing charcoal. The wood has traditionally been used for cogwheels and butchers' chopping blocks. It has also been used to make the striking hammer in pianos.

It is identified in winter by distinctive papery seeds hang in tiered clusters through autumn. Leaf buds are pressed closely to the twig. It is often used in the making of tools, especially on the sole plate of wooden planes. In the past, Hornbeam was used in the production of charcoal as well as being a source of excellent firewood. This is evident from the number of pollarded Hornbeams in Epping Forest, relics of the times when common fuelwood rights existed there.

Hornbeam encourages us to be confident and to open up to movement and change both physically and intellectually. It brings positivity to break free of any self-imposed limiting ideas that prevent us from chasing our dreams.

The genus name *Carpinus*, comes from the Celtic word *carr* (wood) and *pin* (head or nail). The wood of Hornbeam was used to make gears and pegs for waterwheels and windmills. Hornbeam helps the wheels go round! Romans used Hornbeam to make their chariots because of the strength of the wood. Hornbeam leaves were traditionally used to stop bleeding and heal wounds.

The inner bark is used as an emetic and purgative. The bark is astringent, and when boiled up, is used to bathe sore muscles. A tonic can be made from Hornbeam that is said to relieve tiredness and exhaustion. An infusion of the bark can be held in the mouth to relieve the pain of toothache. It is also used as a herbal steam bath in the treatment of rheumatism.

In myths from around the world, trees like Hornbeam appear as ladders between worlds, as sources of life and wisdom, and as the physical forms of supernatural beings. Some myths report that this is an immortal tree with the ability to live forever. Fossil fruits of Hornbeam have been extracted from borehole samples of the Middle Miocene fresh water deposits in Nowy Sacz Basin, Poland. It is a very ancient tree.

Trunk

Here is a practice for you to set up working with your everyday senses with the tree. With Hornbeam you are going to be working with your sense of sight.

Find a Hornbeam tree or take a twig from a branch from the Hornbeam in your hands. Position yourself so that you can view the tree or the branch closely and for some time. Take some time to breathe and come into the present. Connect with the spirit of this tree by sensing its living form in front of you or through holding the branch in your hands. When you feel you have a sense of connection with one another, thank the Hornbeam for opening to you and ask it if it would be a soul mirror for you.

Now spend some time carefully watching the form of the tree or the twig from a branch. Be aware of the tree's aesthetic and beauty. As you take in the aesthetic and beauty of the Hornbeam, allow this to be the aesthetic and beauty of you too. As you connect with the beauty of the tree visibly, feel this beauty alive in you. It will be almost like you are drinking the beauty, but actually you are allowing the beauty and aesthetic to be activated in you by the tree as it mirror the beauty of your soul.

Stay like this for about fifteen minutes. Notice what happens for you. Take notes.

Branches

Here are pathways you can take with the tree opening up whilst spending time with it or whilst accessing the realms behind this one in a journey.

The Hornbeam tree offers great optimism. Its message really is about not giving up and about believing in the goodness we each are. It quietly and unfailingly cheerleads our way. Journey to the spirit of the Hornbeam tree either whilst you are sitting with your back to it or in a journey away from the tree. Spend time really feeling this loving belief and encouragement from the Hornbeam. It might be quite emotional and touching for you.

Ask the tree to bring you medicine to help you to believe in yourself or to help you tune in even more deeply to what is really right for you. Perhaps you have been following a path that isn't quite right. Perhaps you have been finding it difficult to prioritise your own path above others. Maybe you suddenly become aware that what you thought was your intention for this book is something completely different.

After a while of feeling a transmission from Hornbeam bringing the medicine through to you, ask Hornbeam to bring you some guidance and insights about happy endings through your life. What does this feel like? What is it like to be in this place? Feel this deeply in your soul and your body now as you are shown these happy endings that happen because of you following your soul's true note. Now ask Hornbeam to show you visions of the best that can come for you by following your dreams. Ask it to reveal to you what keeps you here and nourishes you. Be open to see what is truly married in your soul.

In some time come back. Feel imbued and blessed by your goodness and your own simple and wonderful way of being. Thank Hornbeam for helping you to appreciate this. Write down some notes.

Leaves

This is a healing exercise you can access with the tree that works with the intention you bring to the book. Before you go into this healing exercise, read the intention that you brought to the book. You can read it out loud to the tree or you can hold this intention in your heart.

Sit beneath or stand with the tree, or hold a twig from the tree across the palm of your hand. In this exercise you are going to access the power of your immortal self.

Take some time to be with the tree or the branch. If you have the branch across your palms, then feel the tree in spirit form in front of you. Imagine the ladder that moves between the worlds that this tree has in myth come down from the tree to meet you. Feel its base at your feet. Take some time to attune to the light that this ladder carries. Put your hands on the imaginary ladder in front of you. Be aware that the ladder brings divine healing light from the other worlds and the whole of time to you.

Feel in your body wherever you might be holding feelings of weakness or disillusionment right now. Ask the ladder to bring the light of your immortal self through from all times to these places by pulling the light through your palms. Allow any healing that is indicated to move through your whole being to each of these places. Acknowledge any relief or strengthening that happens within you.

When your body and soul feel met by the flooding of your immortal self through your being, ask to be shown this beautiful healing immortal power moving into the field of the intention you are holding for this book.

After about twenty minutes, come back to your everyday self and take some notes.

Seeds

Here you take the seeds from the tree to seed your own creativity through story. The seeds of the Hornbeam are distinctive long nuts that hang in clusters even through the winter. Hold the nuts in your hand wither in real life or by calling in their spirit. You are going to connect with an ancestor through your family lines who has held on, endured and lived through a lot of happening to a really happy ending.

Tune into this ancestor and imagine that by holding the nuts in your hand, in life or in spirit, you are holding hands with the ancestor. Let the ancestor take you by the hand and walk you through her or his story, showing you an epic story of how holding on and believing led to a happy ending.

When you come back, thank the Hornbeam for helping you make this connection with your ancestor. Write down the ancestor's story as it was told or as a story or poem inspired by what you were shown. Call it 'The Legend of...' You can start your story with the words 'You never let go, did you? You just kept holding on...'

Questions to complete

1. What is Hornbeam to you?
2. What did Hornbeam show you?
3. What did Hornbeam change in you?
4. How will you do things differently after your work with Hornbeam?
5. How will you work with Hornbeam in your work with others?

Now tune into Hornbeam as you drum and thank it for its time with you and know that you can connect with it at any time. You are ready to work with a new tree.

Chapter 10

Sequoia

The ancestral Sequoias began their existence in Europe, parts of China and Western North America and were well established in the late Cretaceous period. The oldest known giant Sequoia is three and a half thousand years old based on dendrochronology. Giant Sequoias are among the oldest living beings on earth. Comparisons among fossils and modern organisms suggest that by this period Sequoia ancestors had already evolved a greater diameter that allowed it to reach the great heights characteristic of the modern *Sequoiadendron semperverins* (coast redwood) and *Sequoiadendron gigantium* (giant Sequoia). Sequoia is an ancient and majestic tree. Its proximity to the heavens likens it to the hawk's medicine of mastery and perspective.

Giant Sequoia specimens are the most massive individual

trees in the world. They grow to an average height of fifty to eighty five metres, with trunk diameters ranging from six to eight metres. Record trees have been measured at ninety-four point eight metres tall.

Giant Sequoia's bark is fibrous, furrowed, and may be ninety centimetres thick at the base of its columnar trunk. The bark provides significant protection from fire damage. The leaves are evergreen, awl-shaped, three to six millimetres long, and arranged spirally on the shoots.

The giant Sequoia regenerates by its seed. Seed cones are four to seven centimetres long and can mature in eighteen to twenty months. However, they typically remain green and closed for as long as twenty years. Some seeds shed when the cone scales shrink during hot weather in late summer, but most are liberated by insect damage or when the cone dries from the heat of fire. Young trees start to bear cones after twelve years.

Trees may produce sprouts from their stumps subsequent to injury, until about twenty years old; however, shoots do not form on the stumps of mature trees as they do on coast redwoods. Giant Sequoias of all ages may sprout from their boles when branches are lost to fire or breakage. A large tree may have as many as eleven thousand cones. Cone production is greatest in the upper portion of the canopy. A mature giant Sequoia disperses an estimated three to four hundred thousand seeds annually. The winged seeds may fly as far as one hundred and eighty metres from the parent tree.

Right now, give yourself ten minutes to read through this chapter. See if you can spend five minutes quietly attuning or drumming or rattling to ask to connect with the tree in spirit. Feel out into the earth around you for any trees of this species on the land.

Working with Sequoia

First you need to find a Sequoia tree! If you can't reach one easily see if you can take a bit of a branch from a Sequoia you find. You can ask the tree if it is willing to give you a small twig or see if there is one fallen to the ground. You can also work with seeds or leaves/needles or a bit of its bark. Any part of the tree is good. You will now be working through this material with the tree parts to really get to know this tree:

Roots: This is the lore and it gives you information on the qualities that the tree you are working with you is renowned for holding.

Trunk: Here is a practice for you to set up working with your everyday senses with the tree.

Branches: Here are pathways you can take with the tree opening up whilst spending time with it or whilst accessing the realms behind this one in a journey.

Leaves: This is a healing exercise you can access with the tree that works with the intention you bring to the book.

Seeds: Here you take the seeds from the tree to seed your own creativity through story.

Roots
Sequoia's Lore

Britain was introduced to the Sequoia by William Lobb. It was in 1852, that Lobb visited San Francisco and he first heard of mammoth conifers in the foothills of California's Sierra Nevada range. He found about ninety towering. Lobb collected seed, shoots, and seedlings. In fewer than two years' time these would give rise to thousands of saplings, snatched up by wealthy Victorians to adorn great British estates.

The larger-than-life conifer, so symbolic of the vast American wilderness, suddenly became a status symbol in Britain. The Sequoia Gigantea is immune from everything except lightning or fire, and the hand of man. The wood is seemingly everlasting, though brittle and without much strength. Fallen trees after being covered for hundreds of years were found to be in perfect condition.

The known age of the Sequoia Gigantea logged, is usually from eleven to three thousand one hundred years. John Muir, a naturalist states in his book "The Yosemite" that he found one in Kings River Park which was thirty-five and eight-tenths feet in diameter inside the bark four feet above the ground; and by laying bare a section of the charred surface from the heart to bark he counted over four thousand rings.

These monarchs of our planet have witnessed and passed time with so much. They are like the carriers of ancient wisdom. Fossils of the Sequoia Gigantea have been found in the arctic regions of Canada and in Europe. The Sequoia Gigantea of the Sierra Nevada and their cousins, the Sequoia Sempervirens of the Coast Range are merely remnants of a once great forest of earlier geological period. At present they are found nowhere else except in California.

A day in the presence of these trees passes quickly. In each moment one becomes able to appreciate their singular beauty and the miracle of their existence. To be in harmony with them is to be living with grace. Spending time with Sequoia can promote patience. You can almost feel the eloquent lessons they speak, and in a simple following of that divine law set in all our hearts, be also attuned to reaching upward. Sequoia brings a sense of perspective. It can listen to deep aches in the body and alleviate stress and reduce over stimulation of organs and excess production of mucous. Its medicine is to rejuvenate and assist concentration. It helps vision and sooths the pace of those who grow quickly.

It's not easy for a Sequoia seedling to survive. When the seed has just sprouted, it can be eaten by insects, or killed by drought or high heat. Even up to four hundred years, the tree may not thrive, due to lack of sunlight. It probably produces seeds so prolifically to improve the odds that some seeds will grow into a mature tree. In terms of bone health, Sequoia stimulates osteogenesis in both men and women and helps counter osteoporosis and slow bone consolidation in addition to treating glass bone disease.

The Sequoia are technically immortal as their root stock never dies and keeps sprouting new trees of the same genetic stock. Because of their acridity trees are almost immune to moulds that cause wood rot. They have such a thick bark that they are protected from forest fires. The other reason ensuring their long life is that they reproduce from sprouts that spring from the trunk. The young trees can be often seen around the old trunks, giving it better start than seedlings. They are also the fastest growing; there is no phase of old age, in the ordinary sense. Death comes if being cut down or falling down because of their tallness and having their roots too shallow in the soil. The wood is used for carpentry and furniture.

Trunk

Here is a practice for you to set up working with your everyday senses with the tree. For Sequoia, listen to the tree. Put your ear to its trunk and listen deeply. What does it have to tell you? Ask the tree questions and then press your ear to its bark again and listen to what its old deep tall soul has to tell you. Visualise the Sequoia infusing you with its wisdom and bringing strength and calm for your purpose.

Branches

Here are pathways you can take with the tree opening up whilst spending time with it or whilst accessing the realms behind this one in a journey.

Find yourself with the Sequoia or with a part of it you have been gifted. Feel an orb of light around you and set the intention that you take on nothing in this journey and are only available to meet the spirit of the Sequoia tree. Put your hands on the tree or tree part and imagine you go inside the tree. If you are holding just a twig imagine the rest of the tree in front of you. Now ask to attune to the spirit of the tree and ask them to take you to the in-between worlds they reside in. What do you find here? Ask the spirit of the tree to show you its medicine. Ask to be shown how the tree communicates and how we humans can attune better to its energy and its ways. Ask if you can do something to support its role in life.

Leaves

This is a healing exercise you can access with the tree that works with the intention you bring to the book. Before you go into this healing exercise, read the intention that you brought to the book. You can read it out loud to the tree or you can hold this intention in your heart.

Lie under the Sequoia tree or put a twig or part of the tree on your chest. Take some breaths and let yourself feel this great tree energetically attuning to you and your whole self energetically attuning to it. Now hold what feels significant about your intention for the book in your heart. Ask that the tree can deeply listen to this as you come to the end of the book now.

Think about your intention and how you have travelled with it with these ten trees. Feel the Sequoia as part of the family of the oldest living beings on this earth. Ask that the intention you have brought to this book and the bigger plan of the planet can have a meeting together through your connection with Sequoia today. Feel your intention drinking in the bigger plan of the planet. Feel how your intention is held within the bigger plan. Allow your own knowing and truth, your own calling and feeling of what is important for you be acknowledged by this steady, confident and ancient being. Feel yourself and what is important to you being deeply blessed and accepted. Honour the Sequoia and everything that it is so it can feel deeply appreciated and blessed by you too.

After about fifteen minutes, come back to your everyday self and take some notes.

Seeds

Here you take the seeds from the tree to seed your own creativity through story. The giant Sequoias can have as many as eleven thousand cones that house seeds. Feel into the potency of the Sequoia to produce future seeds. Think about the will to survive and also the knowing that not every seed will sprout or survive.

Compare this with your own life. What seeds have you creatively produced that have not grown? What seeds have grown into something significant for you? Make two lists. One is for the seeds that didn't grow into anything and the other is for the ones that did. What does this feel like seeing these two lists written down?

Hold a cone from the Sequoia in your hand (either in real life or in a journey). Feel this cone as one of the cones that produces the seed that will turn into something great and long lasting like the Sequoia tree. Tune into this seed. Feel this seed as being the seed of the intention that you have brought to this book. Feel this seed as the creativity that is closest to your own unique vibration. Understand the seed as the part of you that you were born to bring into life to leave something important and enduring for the planet and for humans. Take time to attune to the preciousness and the incredibleness of this. As you do this, acknowledge the presence of the Ancient ones, the giant Sequoia and the spirits that are connected with them. Feel the immense power and belief in you and your longing to create and bring effectiveness that they carry.

In time, bring your ideas to paper to write a short story or poem called 'A new world was born today'. Write this going into the future with the tree and seeing the vision you hold brought to life. Know that in this writing you are bringing fact through from fiction. Ask the tree to be your guide and walk you through your seed's growth and becoming.

Questions to complete

1. What is Sequoia to you?
2. What did Sequoia help you to understand?
3. What did Sequoia say to you?
4. How do you feel different after your work with Sequoia?
5. How will you work with Sequoia in your work with others?

Now tune into Sequoia as you drum and thank it for its time with you and know that you can connect with it at any time.

Epilogue

Spelling with Trees

Ten trees have been our teachers on this journey! *Trees are our Letters* brings a new kind of spelling to life. Perhaps along the way of this path, we have unconsciously undone a few spells too! Maybe we have enabled a reconnection to the wisdom of nature that could otherwise have passed us by?

I wonder if you will continue to be open to connect with the soul and the creative abilities of other trees in this way now? Maybe when inspiration comes to you on a walk in the woods, you will pause a while and reflect on whether one of the trees is helping an opening in your consciousness.

For we are but a piece of this creative wonder that is life. We are each a singular voice, but also a member of a far greater web, connected especially by the trees. Trees are our original letters. They speak through us all the time. I hope this book can help open up the rich potential of thinking, talking, writing and sound making with the trees on this planet in these times. I hope our neighbours, the trees, can feel us opening to speak more for a world that can be consciously inclusive of them and the whole of nature. When we pause to listen and hear the trees in our letters, perhaps we arrive at the simple truth that we are nature too.

About the Author

Carol Day is an International Visionary Teacher, Artist and Author. She lives in Scotland, UK, where she directs 'Creative Earth Ensemble'– an innovative Arts project. She is the creator of several nature-led models that bring great effectiveness for students, clients, organisations and readers. With an MFA in Fine Art in Context and an MSc in Counselling, Carol contributes to contemporary research. As Psychotherapist, Constellation Facilitator and Shamanic Operator, she runs a successful private practice in Systemic Story Therapy. In 2000, she was one of Scotland's chosen artists for The Year of the Artist. In 2007 she co-designed the Nature as Teacher model for Scotland's first outdoor nursery which has won several awards. She has featured on Radio 4, Blues and Roots Radio and the British Autoethnography conference. Commissioned to generate ground breaking visionary Story programmes working with inclusive community ethos and land, she was the presenter of the 2020 film 'Story of Tatha'.

MOON
BOOKS

PAGANISM & SHAMANISM

What is Paganism? A religion, a spirituality, an alternative belief system, nature worship? You can find support for all these definitions (and many more) in dictionaries, encyclopaedias, and text books of religion, but subscribe to any one and the truth will evade you. Above all Paganism is a creative pursuit, an encounter with reality, an exploration of meaning and an expression of the soul. Druids, Heathens, Wiccans and others, all contribute their insights and literary riches to the Pagan tradition. Moon Books invites you to begin or to deepen your own encounter, right here, right now.

If you have enjoyed this book, why not tell other readers by posting a review on your preferred book site.

Recent bestsellers from Moon Books are:

Journey to the Dark Goddess
How to Return to Your Soul
Jane Meredith
Discover the powerful secrets of the Dark Goddess and transform your depression, grief and pain into healing and integration.
Paperback: 978-1-84694-677-6 ebook: 978-1-78099-223-5

Shamanic Reiki
Expanded Ways of Working with Universal Life Force Energy
Llyn Roberts, Robert Levy
Shamanism and Reiki are each powerful ways of healing; together, their power multiplies. *Shamanic Reiki* introduces techniques to help healers and Reiki practitioners tap ancient healing wisdom.
Paperback: 978-1-84694-037-8 ebook: 978-1-84694-650-9

Pagan Portals – The Awen Alone
Walking the Path of the Solitary Druid
Joanna van der Hoeven
An introductory guide for the solitary Druid, *The Awen Alone* will accompany you as you explore, and seek out your own place within the natural world.
Paperback: 978-1-78279-547-6 ebook: 978-1-78279-546-9

A Kitchen Witch's World of Magical Herbs & Plants
Rachel Patterson
A journey into the magical world of herbs and plants, filled with magical uses, folklore, history and practical magic. By popular writer, blogger and kitchen witch, Tansy Firedragon.
Paperback: 978-1-78279-621-3 ebook: 978-1-78279-620-6

Medicine for the Soul
The Complete Book of Shamanic Healing
Ross Heaven
All you will ever need to know about shamanic healing and how to
become your own shaman…
Paperback: 978-1-78099-419-2 ebook: 978-1-78099-420-8

Shaman Pathways – The Druid Shaman
Exploring the Celtic Otherworld
Danu Forest
A practical guide to Celtic shamanism with exercises and
techniques as well as traditional lore for exploring the Celtic
Otherworld.
Paperback: 978-1-78099-615-8 ebook: 978-1-78099-616-5

Traditional Witchcraft for the Woods and Forests
A Witch's Guide to the Woodland with Guided Meditations and
Pathworking
Mélusine Draco
A Witch's guide to walking alone in the woods, with guided
meditations and pathworking.
Paperback: 978-1-84694-803-9 ebook: 978-1-84694-804-6

Wild Earth, Wild Soul
A Manual for an Ecstatic Culture
Bill Pfeiffer
Imagine a nature-based culture so alive and so connected,
spreading like wildfire. This book is the first flame…
Paperback: 978-1-78099-187-0 ebook: 978-1-78099-188-7

Naming the Goddess
Trevor Greenfield
Naming the Goddess is written by over eighty adherents and
scholars of Goddess and Goddess Spirituality.
Paperback: 978-1-78279-476-9 ebook: 978-1-78279-475-2

Shapeshifting into Higher Consciousness
Heal and Transform Yourself and Our World with Ancient
Shamanic and Modern Methods
Llyn Roberts
Ancient and modern methods that you can use every day to
transform yourself and make a positive difference in the world.
Paperback: 978-1-84694-843-5 ebook: 978-1-84694-844-2

Readers of ebooks can buy or view any of these bestsellers by
clicking on the live link in the title. Most titles are published in
paperback and as an ebook. Paperbacks are available in traditional
bookshops. Both print and ebook formats are available online.

Find more titles and sign up to our readers' newsletter at
http://www.johnhuntpublishing.com/paganism
Follow us on Facebook at https://www.facebook.com/MoonBooks
and Twitter at https://twitter.com/MoonBooksJHP